ALBION HEIGHTS JUNIOR SCHOOL
45 Lynmont Road
Etobicoke, Ont. M9V 3W9

Writing Sense

Authors
Judith Dubé
Kathy Lewis
Robert Malay
Avon Whittles

Consultant
David Booth

Harcourt Brace & Company, Canada
Toronto • Orlando • San Diego • London • Sydney

Copyright © Harcourt Brace & Company Canada, Ltd.

All rights reserved. No part of this publication may be reproduced or transmitted in any form or by any means, electronic or mechanical, including photocopy, recording, or any information storage and retrieval system, without permission in writing from the publisher. Reproducing passages from this book without such written permission is an infringement of copyright law.

Canadian Cataloguing in Publication Data

Main entry under title:

Writing sense, level 7

Includes index.
ISBN 0-7747-1443-3

1. English language — Composition and exercises — Juvenile literature.
2. Authorship — Juvenile literature. I. Dubé, Judith.

PE1408.W777 1998	808'.042	C97-932203-0

Authors:
Judith Dubé
Calgary Roman Catholic Separate School Board, Alberta
Kathy Lewis
Waterloo County Board of Education, Ontario
Robert Malay
Shelburne County District School Board, Nova Scotia
Avon Whittles
Saskatoon Board of Education, Saskatchewan

Consultant:
David Booth
Faculty of Education, University of Toronto, and Ontario Institute for Studies in Education

Reviewers:
Leonard J. Atwood
Edmonton Public Schools, Alberta
Cheryl Bashutski
Regina Roman Catholic School Board, Division #81, Saskatchewan
Suzanne Harper
Peel Board of Education, Ontario
Nancy Anne Henry
Annapolis Valley Regional School Board, Nova Scotia
Judith Hunter
Scarborough Board of Education, Ontario
Frank McCormick
Vancouver School District #39, British Columbia

Mary Schmid
Kamloops/Thompson School District #9, British Columbia
Lynn Sooley
Lewisporte/Gander School District, Newfoundland
Patricia Marie Spencer
District #8 (Saint John), New Brunswick
Sheila Spencer
Red Deer Catholic Regional Division #39, Alberta
Irene Thiry
St. James-Assiniboia School Division #2, Manitoba
Clevie Wall
Halifax Regional School Board, Nova Scotia
Diane Wilkins
School District #18, New Brunswick
Bev Zizzy
Regina Public School Board, Saskatchewan

Project Manager: Wendy Graham
Supervising Editor: Jennifer Armstrong
Editor: Patrice Peterkin
Manager of Editorial Services: Nicola Balfour
Senior Production Editor: Dianne Broad
Production Manager: Gaynor Fitzpatrick
Production Coordinator: Donna Dowsett
Manager of Art and Design: Dennis Boyes
Design, Art Direction, and Page Composition:
  Sonya V. Thursby/Opus House Incorporated, Danni Stor
Cover Design: Water Street Graphics
Cover Illustrator: Greg Douglas

∞ This book was printed in Canada on acid-free paper.
1 2 3 4 5   01 00 99 98 97

Contents

Getting Started 4

Using This Book 5
The Writing Process 8

Writing Formats (Purposes) 20

Personal Narrative	Journals *(to interpret, reflect, record)*	22
	Mysteries *(to entertain, imagine)*	28
	Fantasy Stories *(to entertain, imagine)*	33
	Pourquoi Tales *(to explain, entertain)*	39
Humour	Jokes *(to entertain, use language creatively)*	45
Research	Research Reports *(to inform, report)*	51
	Surveys *(to inform, report, interpret)*	57
	Profiles *(to inform, report)*	63
Messages	Thank-You Notes *(to inform, inquire)*	71
	Friendly Letters *(to inform, report)*	76
Advertising	Print Advertisements *(to persuade, inform)*	83
	Jingles *(to persuade, entertain)*	89
Poetry	Couplets and Quatrains *(to reflect, entertain)*	95
	Found Poetry *(to interpret, entertain)*	101
Instructions	Rules *(to direct, inform)*	107
Drama	Reader's Theatre Scripts *(to interpret, entertain)*	114
Persuasive	Letters to the Editor *(to persuade, express opinion)*	121
	Speeches *(to persuade, express opinion, inform)*	126

Style File 133

Writing Terms and Techniques 134

Tool Kit 153

Conducting Research 154
Grammar and Usage 160
Punctuation 175
Spelling 181
Word Power 187

Index 191

Getting Started

This book is for you—to help you learn how to write in a variety of creative formats and to develop your skills as a writer. In this book you'll find plenty of opportunities to express your ideas and opinions, use your imagination, report information, develop plots and characters, and experiment with words, rhythm, and writing techniques.

But that isn't all. *Writing Sense* also provides you with a glossary of writing terms and techniques called the **Style File** and a handy reference section called the **Tool Kit** that is full of information on conducting research, grammar and usage, punctuation, spelling, and word power—everything you need to make sense of writing.

So thumb through the book and get comfortable with it. Take note of all the features and information that you find helpful and use them in your writing. Remember, the more you write, the more you'll discover about being a writer. And if you're enjoying what you write, your audience is sure to enjoy it too.

Using This Book

This *Writing Sense* book has ideas for writing in 18 different formats. Each format is divided into sections that take you through the stages of the writing process. (For more about the Writing Process, see pages 8–19.) These same sections appear in each of the 18 formats—that way you'll know where to find the help you need as you write. Here's a description of each section. (Note the special features that give you extra help and information throughout the process.)

Introduction

Each writing format is introduced with a description of the format and an explanation of its various purposes. Thinking about the purpose of the format can help you make decisions about what and how you'll write.

Writing Goals

Every format is different. The writing goals are listed to give you an idea of what you should be focussing on as you write in each format. Take the opportunity to set a few goals for yourself—no one knows what you need to work on to improve your writing as well as you do.

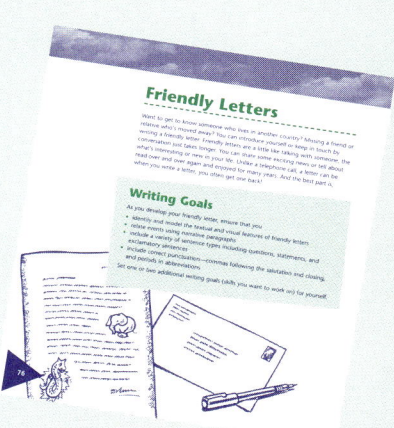

Writing Sample

Each format has a writing sample by a Canadian student your age. You can examine the features of the sample, and use it as a model for your writing. Notice the notes for each sample that highlight some of the important features of it.

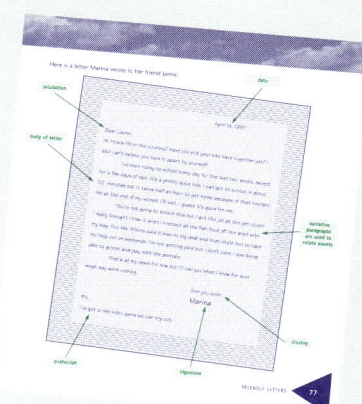

GETTING STARTED 5

Check These Out!

This is a reference list of books and other sources that contain samples of writing in each format.

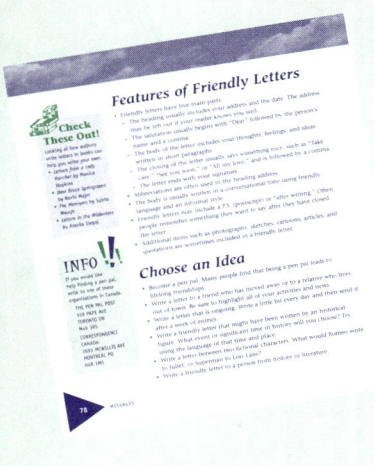

Features

Each format has its own special textual and visual features. These features are explained in this section. You can refer to this list when you are writing. When you are revising, you can check the list to make sure that you've included all the features in your own writing.

Choose an Idea

This section includes several ideas to get you started writing in the format. Some ideas you can do on your own; others might involve a partner or small group. You can use one of these ideas or come up with your own.

Planning

Whichever idea you choose, you'll find helpful suggestions in this section for planning and organizing your ideas. You don't have to follow the steps in the order they are presented. Work in a way that you find comfortable.

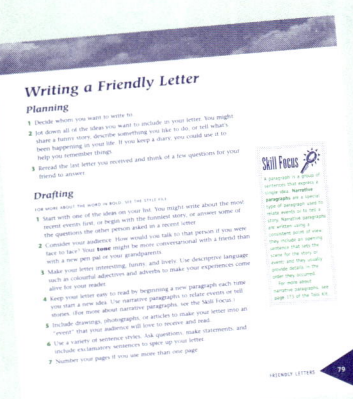

Drafting

This section includes ideas to guide you through writing your first draft. The steps are numbered so you can follow them easily. Remember, you don't have to follow every step. At this point you may find that the idea you've selected isn't working out. You may want to go back to Choose an Idea and try a different one.

Skill Focus

Be sure to check out the Skill Focus feature throughout the formats. This feature has tips for improving your writing as you plan, draft, and revise your formats. The tips also refer you to more information in the **Style File** or **Tool Kit** sections at the back of the book.

Revising

The questions posed in this section can help you revise the content, organization, wording, voice, and style of your writing, and ensure that it has the features of the format.

Editing

Once the content is set you can focus on the mechanics of your writing and look closely at your spelling, grammar and usage, punctuation, and capitalization. You can find helpful tips and information in the **Tool Kit** at the back of the book.

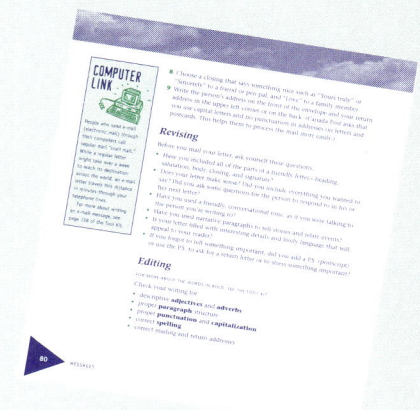

Info

This feature is found throughout the book. Each one contains interesting and helpful information related directly to the formats.

Computer Link

The Computer Links offer information for using the computer as a writing tool—everything from conducting research on the Internet, to specific programs or software, to writing tips related to the computer, to design and formatting suggestions.

Publishing

Not all writing needs to be shared, and not all writing should be published. If you decide to publish your writing, you can share your work with your chosen audience by selecting one of the options in this section. Some ideas involve collaborating with a partner or a group of classmates.

Reflecting

The questions in this section can help you reflect on your writing experience. They can help you to focus on what you've learned about writing and what you found enjoyable or challenging about the format. The questions also encourage you to give some thought to the format itself—is it an effective means for achieving its purpose, and if so, why?

The Writing Process

TIP
Not all writing formats will require you to go through all of these stages. Personal formats—a diary, for example—often have just one draft and generally won't be published.

Each time you begin a new piece of writing you'll probably be faced with questions like What will I write about? and How will I write it? Many writers work through a series of steps or stages called the Writing Process. This process breaks down the work of writing into tasks, making it easier to deal with.

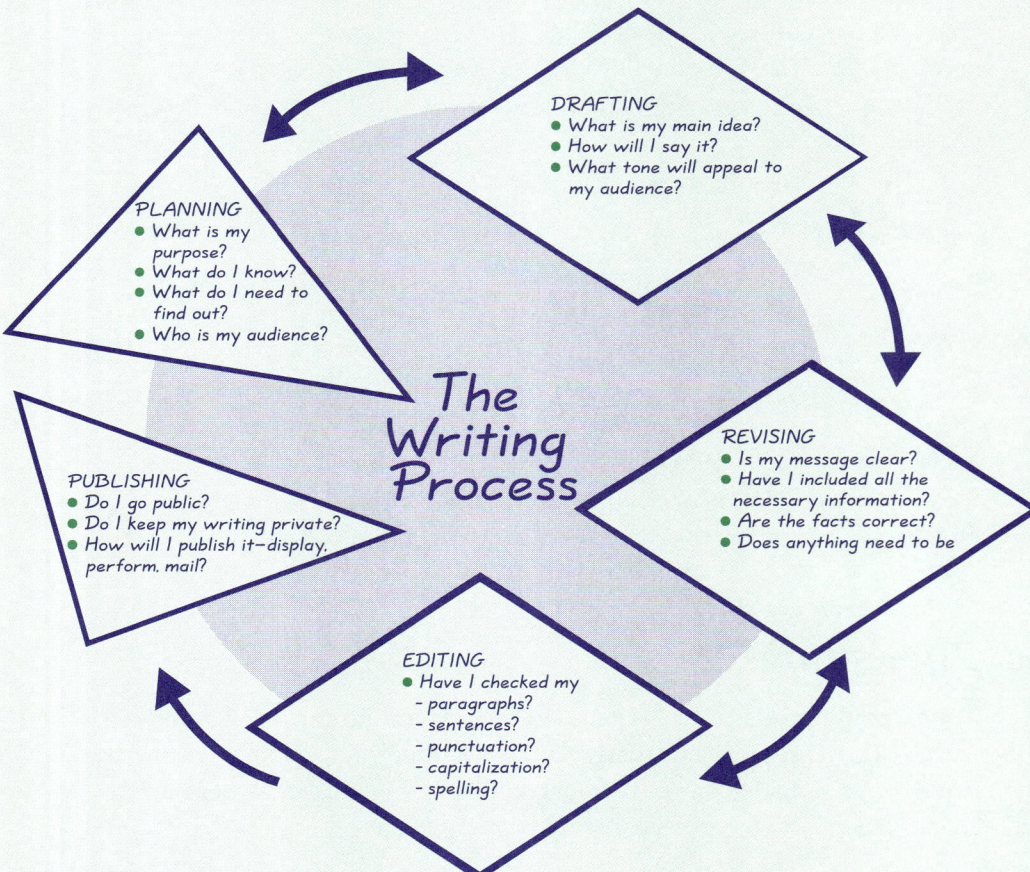

PLANNING
- What is my purpose?
- What do I know?
- What do I need to find out?
- Who is my audience?

DRAFTING
- What is my main idea?
- How will I say it?
- What tone will appeal to my audience?

REVISING
- Is my message clear?
- Have I included all the necessary information?
- Are the facts correct?
- Does anything need to be

EDITING
- Have I checked my
  - paragraphs?
  - sentences?
  - punctuation?
  - capitalization?
  - spelling?

PUBLISHING
- Do I go public?
- Do I keep my writing private?
- How will I publish it—display, perform, mail?

The arrows indicate a natural flow through the stages, but as you become a more experienced writer, you may find there is no real dividing line between the stages. You might work back and forth through the stages. For example, as you discuss the focus of your draft with a classmate, you may find that you need to collect more information, so you might go back to the planning stage.

WRITING SENSE

Planning

The planning stage involves
- thinking
- choosing a subject or writing idea
- exploring the idea
- collecting and organizing information and details
- deciding your purpose, format, and audience

> **TIP**
> If you are assigned topics for your writing, decisions about the format, purpose, and style will already have been made for you.

Searching for Ideas

Ideas for writing come from many sources: they come from observing what is happening around you, from watching people, from what you're reading, conversations with your friends, and experiences you've had. Many writers record their observations, experiences, and thoughts in journals and writing folders. They brainstorm, free write, and use graphic organizers (webs, tree diagrams, and charts) to develop their ideas. Try some of the following ideas as you write in different formats.

Journals and Writing Folders

A journal is a great place to reflect on your thoughts and feelings, and to explore ideas and store them for future use. You can also use a writing folder to store ideas and information you find interesting. You never know when you could weave these ideas into your writing.

Brainstorming

To brainstorm, choose a topic and write it down on a piece of paper, then list every idea that comes to mind about that subject even if it seems silly or unrelated. You can go through later and choose the best ideas. You can brainstorm alone, with a partner, or with a group.

Free Writing

Free writing involves writing down everything as it comes to your mind. Write for three to five minutes without stopping. Free writing can help loosen up your thoughts and let the ideas flow, and may allow you to find a focus for your writing. It can also help you to solve a problem in a draft at the revising stage.

Graphic Organizers

Graphic organizers—webs, diagrams, charts—are visual ways of organizing thoughts and ideas. You put words into the shapes created by the lines, circles, and boxes.

WEBS

A web is used to develop details, or to narrow a topic. This is how you web.

- Write a word or phrase summarizing an idea in the centre of a page and draw a circle around it.
- Surround the idea with related ideas. Circle these, and draw lines connecting each new idea to the original one.
- Add more ideas as they come to mind.
- Keep going until you can't think of any more connections.

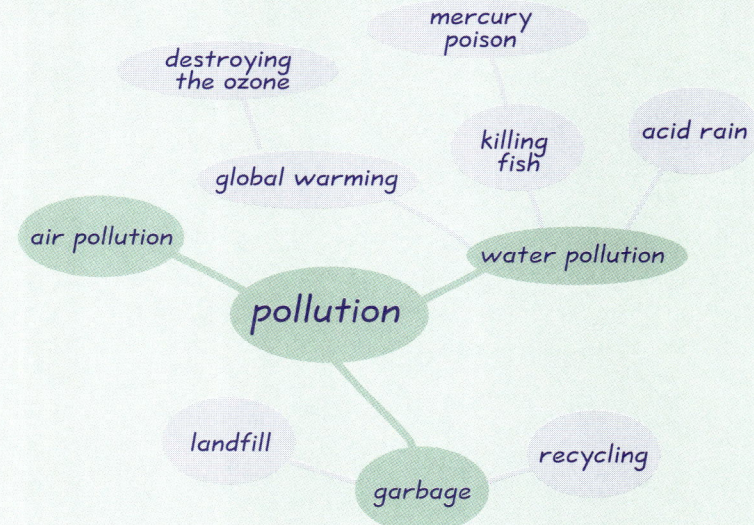

TREE DIAGRAMS

To see how ideas connect to each other, try a tree diagram.

- Write your main topic in the centre of the diagram.
- Place smaller key ideas or supporting details in headings that stem from the centre of the diagram.
- Then link even smaller headings and more detailed information to the key ideas until your diagram looks like a tree with many branches. Check out these two tree diagrams.

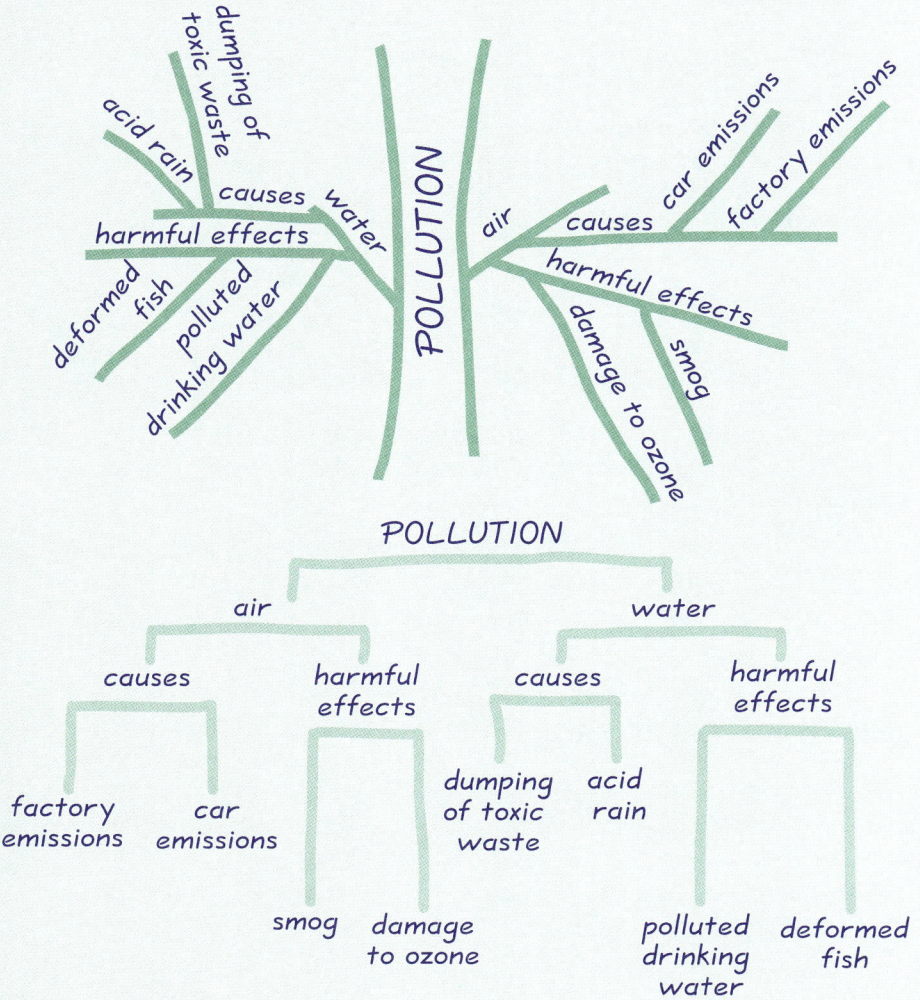

GETTING STARTED 11

CHARTS

Putting your information in charts can help you determine what you already know from what you need to find out about a topic. A chart is a good place to start before you conduct research. Set up a page with three columns titled What I Know About the Topic, What I Need to Find Out, and Where I Can Get the Information, and then fill in the columns.

Topic — Pollution

What I Know About the Topic	What I Need to Find Out	Where I Can Get the Information
- ozone being destroyed - global warming - pollution affects the ecosystem - recycling helps to reduce garbage in landfills	- what the causes are - how pollution affects the air - harmful effects on people - what we can do to stop pollution	- library - CD-ROMs - Internet

Choosing and Developing a Topic

Sort through the ideas you've developed so far in your journals, charts, or webs. Choose a topic—one that you feel committed to or that you want to learn more about. Then, consider the following points as you develop your topic.

- Narrow the focus. For example, if you've chosen pollution, you might narrow your focus to air pollution or the effects of air pollution.
- Collect information. You may need to conduct research. (See Conducting Research on pages 154–159 of the Tool Kit.)

Purpose, Format, Audience, Voice

Once you've developed an idea, you'll need to make decisions about the purpose of your piece, its format, your audience, and the voice you'll use. Keep in mind that a piece of writing can have more than one purpose. You may write a profile to inform and entertain your audience, for example. Consider the following questions.

Purpose
- Are you writing to explain, to instruct, to persuade, to reflect, to entertain, or to interpret?
- How will your purpose affect which format you choose?

Format
- Which format would work best with your topic and your purpose?
 For example, if you want to persuade people that the effects of air pollution are harmful, you might choose to write a speech or a persuasive essay.

Audience
- For whom are you writing? Classmates? Family members? Yourself? Your community?
- How will your audience affect what you write? What might they already know or what might they need to know?

Voice
Your audience also helps you to determine the voice you will use. Voice is made up of the tone (formal, informal) and your writing style (the way you write sentences and put your ideas together).
- Will your writing be serious, funny, or friendly?
- How will it make your audience feel?
- Will you use short sentences and simple language, or a mix of long and short sentences with technical terminology?

Writing an Outline

An outline is a short-form summary of what you plan to write. Outlines help you to organize your ideas, and most important, they give you a place to start writing. You can develop your outline by hand or on computer. As you compose on the computer, keep a copy of your outline beside you and refer to it often.

Report Outline

Main Idea
1. Supporting idea
   a. detail
      - minor detail
      - minor detail
   b. detail
      - minor detail
      - minor detail
2. Supporting idea
   a. detail
      - minor detail
      - minor detail

Story Outline

Characters

Setting

Plot
- event 1
- event 2
- event 3

GETTING STARTED

Setting Up Your Draft

Setting up your draft in the following way will give you room on your page to do any revising that is needed. It will also help you keep track of your progress.

- Stamp "first draft" or "second draft" on your paper and date it.
- Number your pages. For drafts on computer, use a header for the page numbers and date.
- Write on one side of the paper only.
- Leave wide margins.
- Double-space your draft.

TIP

If you're using a computer, be sure to save often—about every 10 minutes—and back up copies on floppy disks. Remember, disks are durable but *can* be damaged by dropping or improper storage.

Drafting

This is where you first start writing down or "drafting" your ideas in sentence form on paper or on the computer in a way that makes sense to you. Write freely, recording all your ideas. This initial writing is called a first draft and it does not have to be perfect.

- If you get stuck in one section of your piece, skip to another and come back to it later.
- If your writing stops, go back to your outline and pick up a new idea to get your draft going again.
- Try accordion writing. Write the main headings or key phrases from your outline in capital letters, and start writing under any heading. Any time you run out of ideas, move to a new heading and start writing.
- Begin with opening sentences that grab the readers' attention so they'll want to read the rest of the piece. However, the opening sentences may not be the first thing that you write. Sometimes writers jump into the middle of a piece, then go back and write the opening.

OPENING SENTENCES

Try one of the following techniques to begin your piece.

- Share a short story.
- Begin with a surprising fact.
- Begin with an interesting quotation.
- Start with dialogue.
- Begin a story in the middle of the action.
- Introduce a few of the main points.
- Use the 2-3-1 principle: put the second most important point at the beginning of the paragraph, the least important point in the middle, and the most important point at the end.

WRITING SENSE

THE MIDDLE AND THE END
Stay on track. All of the ideas in the body of your writing should support or explain your subject. If you're writing a narrative, the body should move the action along.
- *Maintain your voice—keep your tone and style consistent throughout your draft.*
- *At the end, sum up the main idea and then restate the importance of your topic. It should be as strong and as powerful as your opening.*

Revising

Revising refers to all the changes you make to your draft to improve it. You can change a word or whole sections; move, add, or cut information; or rework the main idea, the tone, or the purpose. (See the Style File for information on writing techniques you might include.) Consider these suggestions as you revise.

- Read what you've written and revise for one aspect of writing, such as logical order. Then go through it again, keeping another aspect in mind.
- Instead of telling your readers what to see, think, or feel, allow them to come to the conclusion you want by showing them. Appeal to their senses with descriptive language. For example:

  TELLING *My sister plays her drums a lot.*

  SHOWING *Almost every night, I can hear the pounding beat of my sister's drums as she bangs away.*
- Consider the voice (tone and style) you've used. Is it suitable for your purpose, your audience, and the format you've chosen?
- If you're working on computer, print out each revision so that you can see how your changes affect the piece. Even experienced writers find it hard to revise on screen without printing out a hard copy.
- Hold a peer conference with a partner or a small group to discuss your writing. Working with a partner or small group to revise each other's work can help you make sense of your thoughts and ideas. You'll also get opinions about what is strong or weak in your drafts. At this point, you should concentrate on the ideas and flow of the writing.

Peer Conference Tips

- Focus on one aspect of the draft at a time.
- Read the draft for content.
- Look at how the piece is organized.
- Make suggestions, but allow the writers to decide what changes they want to make.
- Remember that the author "owns" the writing and makes the decisions about it.

Editing Symbols

Check out these editing symbols and use them to "mark up" your writing to show the changes you need to make.

- ⌃ add a comma
- ⌃ add a colon
- ⌃ add a period
- ⌃ add a semicolon
- ⌃ insert (put in)
- ¶ new paragraph
- ∼ transpose (change the order)
- ⌿ delete (take out)
- ╱ lower-case letter
- ≡ capital letter
- ⌒ move text

Editing

Once you've revised and are satisfied with the content of your draft, concentrate on the mechanics of your work—the sentence structure, paragraph breaks, grammar, punctuation, spelling, and so on. This is called editing and it refers to all the final changes you make to a piece. During this step you polish your style and put the finishing touches on your writing. All your sentences should read smoothly and be free from obvious errors such as spelling mistakes.

Check for only one aspect at a time. You might choose a specific area that you need help with and ask a classmate to check it for you. (See the Tool Kit for more information on the mechanics of writing.)

Many computer software programs have a spell checker, a grammar checker, and a thesaurus. Use these tools, but remember that the computer can't do the thinking for you. You will need to decide what to change.

Publishing

Publishing refers to the ways of presenting a finished or good copy of your writing. If you decide to share your work and are satisfied that your piece is the best you can make it, you're ready to go public with your writing. Whichever method you choose for publishing your work—reading it aloud, entering a contest, or sending it to the local paper—the point is to let your audience share in what you have written. Work that is shared with an audience should be error-free.

Keep in mind that a computer opens up a lot of publishing possibilities. You can arrange a poem in a dramatic way, print out a newspaper article in a two-column format for a professional look, or even send an e-mail message through the Internet.

When formatting on the computer, use readable computer fonts or type faces. Experiment with different type sizes to indicate the importance of headings. Carefully consider using bold, outline, shadow, or italic type. Used sparingly they add interest, but using too many type styles makes your writing cluttered and confusing.

Working With the Process

Once you understand what to focus on at each stage of the Writing Process, your writing should improve. Being aware of what to do at each stage allows you to focus on only those tasks. Here is an example of one piece of writing that has been taken through the Writing Process.

Drafting

This is the first draft of Daniel's story.

My ship the Bluenose II was set to sail. My crew of thirty men, was all strong and willing for adventure. A crowd had gathered at the dock to see us depart.

"Catch the beast," they kept calling. We cast off and as the shore grew fainter, the wind and waves grew stronger. Bluenose was a fine ship. She was made of the finest wood, and Johansen took care of her so fondly. She was at least a hundred feet long, nothing but thirty feet wide, and her mast stood a hundred feet into the sky.

For weeks we searched. My crew was becoming anxious and alarmed that we would not find it, and that we would be forced back without a prize. If we didn't find it within the next week we would have to turn back.

I was in my chamber when it hapened. I scrambled out of my cabin an onto to the deck. There was panic all over the ship and I shouted and shouted for them to calm down. The beast was enormous, much bigger and more menacing than I had thought. The body of this beast was twice the size of our ship, and it swam like nothing I had seen before. It raised its head above the sea as high as our mast. The neck was thick as a tree, and the body was submerged under the water. Its tentacles spread and covered the water like vines. The water was dark and dense, and it became clear to me that it was slowly swimming towards us.

Suddenly the whole neck and head lowered itself into the water and it vanished, sending out deafening waves. I saw a black solid mass firing through the water straight towards us. I spun around to my crew. I roared at them to arm themselves and the boat. They scrambled and took out all sorts of guns and spears. The cannons were armed and aimed, and I stood tall at the side of the boat. Suddenly its head rose in front of me. The body was fifty metres away and the head, large as my room, smashed against the side of the ship. I bellowed to my crew to fire, and they did. I lay down against the deck and loaded my shotgun. The head flew across the deck, not teen feet above myself, smashing through the main mast, and I yelled in outrage. Suddenly the head snapped back and flew at

Ramirez. It was like the shadow of a snake killing a mouse. A black mass of tentacles shook the ship and I shot away at the beast. Oily dark blood escaped from the hoard, and I shot again, but the beast kept picking off my men one by one. I finally cried abandon ship as the monster tore it apart.

* * * * * * * * * *

I had been beached on a small island for I knew not how long. My whole crew was gone. I spent a few days on the island searching for food and building a raft. I rigged it with food and supplies, then set sail. I had spent the night before studying the stars and I was able to determine the direction back to the mainland. By the third week out, I was fainting every other hour weak from a lack of water. I knew I could not last much longer. The sun rose, cruel as ever on one particular day. It was then that I saw it again. The monster lay straight in front of me close enough that I could hear it breathing. The raft came to rest near the beast. My raft was so small in comparison to the beast, that it didn't seem to notice me. Suddenly in the distance I could see a ship. It was twice the size of the Bluenose had been. They had sent another ship out to hunt for the beast. Realizing my peril, I used my hands to paddle quickly away from the beast. The size of the ship seemed to intimidate the beast, because it suddenly dove out of sight and disapeared. I began to wave my hands and yell with the last ounce of my strength. A boat was row boat lowered and I was rescued. As I was helped on board I couldn't help but think that the beast had been my savior. If another ship hadn't been sent out after it, I would never have been found.

Revising

These notes were made after a conference with a classmate to discuss the content.

I was already an old man when it hapened, and now as I write this, I can only faintly remember how it all hapened. Of course you must know my name by now. It swept the world. Wherever I go, people gather around me and ask about my adventure. and the

My ship the Bluenose II was set to sail. My crew of thirty men was all strong and willing for adventure. A crowd had gathered at the dock to see us depart.

"Catch the beast," they kept calling. We cast off, and as the shore grew fainter, the wind and waves grew stronger. Bluenose was a fine ship. She was made of the finest wood, and Johansen took care of her so fondly. She was at least a hundred feet long, nothing but thirty feet wide, and her mast stood a hundred feet into the sky.

For weeks we searched. My crew was becoming anxious and alarmed that we would not find it, and that we would be forced back without a prize. If we didn't find it within the next week we would have to turn back.

I was in my chamber when it happened. I scrambled out of my cabin an onto to the deck. There was panic all over the ship and I shouted and shouted for them to calm down. The beast was Its enormous, much bigger and more menacing than I had thought. The body of this beast was twice the size of our ship, and it swam like nothing I had seen before. It raised its head above the sea as high as our mast. The neck was thick as a tree, and the body was submerged under the water. Its tentacles spread and covered the water like vines. The water was dark and dense, and it became clear to me that it was slowly swimming towards us.

Suddenly the whole neck and head lowered itself into the water and it vanished, sending out deafening waves. I saw a black solid mass firing through the water straight towards us. I spun around to my crew, I roared at them to arm themselves and the boat. They scrambled and took out all sorts of guns and spears. The cannons were armed and aimed, and I stood tall at the side of the boat. Suddenly its head rose in front of me. The body was fifty metres away and the head, large as my room, smashed against the side of the ship. I bellowed to my crew to fire, and they did. I lay down against the deck and loaded my shotgun. The head flew across the deck, not ten feet above myself, smashing through the main mast, and I yelled in outrage. Suddenly the head snapped back and flew at

Ramirez. It was like the shadow of a snake killing a mouse. A black mass of tentacles shook the ship and I shot away at the beast. Oily dark blood escaped from the hoard, and I shot again, but the beast kept picking off my men one by one. I finally cried abandon ship as the monster tore it apart.

The scarlet sky wept rays of sunshine down upon my skin.
I had been beached on a small island for I knew not how long. My whole crew was gone. I spent a few days on the island searching for food and building a raft. I rigged it with food and supplies, then set sail. I had spent the night before studying the stars and I was able to determine the direction back to the mainland. By the third week out, I was fainting every other hour weak from a lack of water. I knew I could not last much longer. The sun rose, cruel as ever on one particular day. It was then that I saw it again. The monster lay straight in front of me close enough that I could hear it breathing. The raft came to rest near the beast. My raft was so small in comparison to the beast, that it didn't seem to notice me. Suddenly in the distance I could see a ship. It was twice the size of the Bluenose had been. They had sent another ship out to hunt for the beast. Realizing my peril, I used my hands to paddle quickly away from the beast. The size of the ship seemed to intimidate the beast, because it suddenly dove out of sight and disapeared. I began to wave my hands and yell with the last ounce of my strength. A boat was row boat lowered and I was rescued. As I was helped on board I couldn't help but think that the beast had been my savior. If another ship hadn't been sent out after it, I would never have been found.

Editing

After making changes to content, Daniel looked at individual sentences, paragraphs, grammar, and checked the spelling.

I was already an old man when it happened, and now as I write this, I can only faintly remember how it all happened. Of course you must know my name by now. Wherever I go, people gather around me and ask about my adventure.

My ship the Bluenose II was set to sail and the crew of thirty men was all strong and ready willing for adventure. A crowd had gathered at the dock to see us depart. "Catch the beast," they kept calling. The Bluenose was a fine ship. Made of the finest wood, she was at least a hundred feet long, thirty feet wide, and her mast stood a hundred feet into the sky. We cast off, and as the shore grew fainter, the wind and waves grew stronger.

For weeks we searched. My crew was becoming anxious and alarmed that we would not find the beast, and that we would be forced back without our prize.

I was in my chamber when it happened. I scrambled out of my cabin and onto to the deck. There was panic all over the ship and I shouted and shouted for them to calm down. The beast was enormous, much bigger and more menacing than I had thought. Its body was twice the size of our ship, and it swam like nothing I had seen before. It raised its head above the sea as high as our mast. The neck was thick as a tree, and the body was submerged under the water. Its tentacles spread and covered the water like vines. The water was dark and dense as it slowly swam towards us.

Suddenly the beast lowered itself into the water and vanished, sending out deafening waves. I then saw a black solid mass firing through the water straight towards us. Spinning around to my crew, I roared at them to arm themselves. They scrambled and took out all sorts of guns and spears, and armed and aimed the cannons.

With a screeching sound Suddenly its head rose in front of me and smashed against the side of the ship. I bellowed to my crew to fire, and they did. The head flew across the deck, not ten feet above me, smashing through the main mast, and I yelled in outrage. Suddenly the head snapped back and flew at Ramirez. It was like the shadow of a snake killing a mouse. A black mass of tentacles shook the ship and I shot away at the beast until its I kept shooting Oily dark blood splattered onto the deck. I shot again, but the beast kept picking off my men one by one. I finally cried abandon ship as the monster tore it apart.

* * * * * * * * * *

The scarlet sky wept rays of sunshine down upon my skin. I had been beached on a small island for I knew not how long. My whole crew was gone. I spent a few days on the island searching for food and building a raft. I rigged it with food and supplies, then set sail. I had spent the night before studying the stars and I was able to determine the direction back to the mainland.

By the third week out, I was fainting every other hour weak from a lack of water. I knew I could not last much longer. The sun rose, cruel as ever on one particular day. It was then that I saw it again. The monster lay straight in front of me close enough that I could hear it breathing. The raft came to rest near the beast. My raft was so small in comparison to the beast that it didn't seem to notice me. Suddenly in the distance I could see a ship. It was twice the size the Bluenose had been. They had sent another ship out to hunt for the beast. Realizing my peril, I used my hands to paddle quickly away from the beast. The size of the ship seemed to intimidate the beast, because it suddenly dove out of sight and disappeared. I began to wave my hands and yell with the last ounce of my strength. A rowboat was lowered and I was rescued. As I was helped on board I couldn't help but think that the beast had been my savior. If another ship hadn't been sent out after it, I would never have been found.

Final Draft

Daniel added a title to his story, and then printed out a clean final draft.

GETTING STARTED 19

Writing Formats

Writing formats are different types of writing that are used for a variety of purposes to appeal to different audiences. Every format is distinct, with specific textual and visual features. For example, a survey (with questions and blank space for the answers) looks nothing like a comic strip (with illustrations) or a persuasive essay (with straight text).

Just as each writing format has special features, each format is used for specific purposes. If you want to persuade your parents that you should have a later curfew, you won't use a thank-you note. An editorial, a friendly letter, or even a testimonial would probably be more effective.

Learning to write in a variety of ways will allow you to choose the best possible format to achieve success, no matter the purpose or the audience.

Personal
- Journals 22

Narrative
- Mysteries 28
- Fantasy Stories 33
- Pourquoi Tales 39

Humour
- Jokes 45

Research
- Research Reports 51
- Surveys 57
- Profiles 63

Messages
- Thank-You Notes 71
- Friendly Letters 76

Advertising
- Print Advertisements 83
- Jingles 89

Poetry
- Couplets and Quatrains 95
- Found Poetry 101

Instructions
- Rules 107

Drama
- Reader's Theatre Scripts 114

Persuasive
- Letters to the Editor 121
- Speeches 126

Personal

• *Journals*

When you think of personal writing you probably think about writing in diaries, where you record your feelings and thoughts about people and the events taking place around you. Writing about these things can help you reflect on situations and interpret your feelings and attitudes about these happenings and people. You consider how you feel and what you might do differently next time.

However, personal writing can be much more than diary writing. Keeping a journal, for example, is a wonderful way to keep track of your special interests and hobbies, such as art, nature, or music. You can record information that comes your way, draw sketches and illustrations, and add "bits and pieces," such as photographs, favourite quotations, or cut-out articles.

Personal writing is most successful when it reflects the real you—when it shows the interesting things that make you unique.

Journals

Keeping a journal is a great way to express and record your thoughts, feelings, dreams, and memories. Journals are also a convenient place to make note of interesting things you see, and to collect ideas for stories and poems. Jottings, pictures, articles, quotations, or anything else you find interesting may be included.

With a journal, you have a special place to record, reflect on, and interpret aspects of your life or of the world around you. Recording, writing, or illustrating a journal allows you to be creative and to experiment with ideas, language, and art in a private place that you might decide never to share.

Many people keep a special book for their journals. Others choose to keep their journal on computer, audiotape, or videotape.

Writing Goals

As you develop your journal, ensure that you

- identify and model the features of journal entries
- establish your own voice as a writer
- experiment with sentences and punctuation
- discover the importance and power of reflective writing

Set one or two additional writing goals (skills you want to work on) for yourself.

Chad wrote this entry for a journal of school trips that his class created.

entry is dated → May 15, 1997

On our trip I liked visiting China, Ancient Egypt, and the jungles of South America. We saw a lot there, like wild beasts, ancient scriptures, and camels. Well of course this is too good to be true. But it is...partly true. We only got to see one big building. This was one of the most interesting places we went to on our Toronto trip.

On May 13, I went with my classmates and Mr. Bray, our teacher, on a trip to Toronto. I have a lot of memories from this trip that will be hard to forget. We went to the museum, to the top of the CN Tower, and much more.

First of all the bus—the bus came and everyone got on but...we were missing one person. Okay, I'll give you three choices: A) the bus driver, B) the whole class, or C) Mr. Bray. If you guessed C, you're right! He got there after everyone was on the bus and ready to go.

When we got to Toronto I thought it was funny to see a German Shepherd wandering on a rooftop of a building.

I'll always remember Phil saying, "Hey look, the CN Tower." That tricked a lot of people as they looked out their windows saying, "Where? Where?" He just laughed and said, "Gotcha!"

uses a variety of sentence styles and punctuation

First stop was the Ontario Legislature. Well, I don't have many memories except thinking about the pages. If kids with straight A's go and work there and only get $10 a day, that's not worth their intelligence.

After the Legislature we went into McDonald's for lunch. Whenever I think of McDonald's, I remember my grandma. She is guilty of once spilling orange juice at a Winnipeg McDonald's restaurant. Well you can guess what happened. Not one, but five people spilled their drinks. (How embarrassing!) First Jenna spilled hers on the ground. Then Kirsty, after being bumped by an older man. Then a lady at a nearby table spilled hers, and then Ryan dumped his on a chair. Finally, a guy working the cash register spilled one.

includes reflection and details

After that hilarious experience we went to the Royal Ontario Museum. This is where I visited China, Ancient Egypt, and the jungles of South America. (Pretty lame, huh?) I've never seen so much stuff under one roof...except, maybe, for my room. (Just kidding.) Well it took us about 30 minutes to reach the amazing bat cave but we found it. We actually got Jenna in there even though she says she's scared of bats. She did have a terrified expression on her face the whole time she was in the cave.

Now here's my turn to get beet red. The insect area totally grossed me out!!! After seeing a big hairy tarantula, worms, cockroaches, and stick bugs, boy, I was glad to get out of there.

the writer's voice is unique

JOURNALS 23

Features of Journals

- A journal is a place to record, interpret, and reflect on thoughts, feelings, and experiences.
- Entries are written daily or every few days.
- Each entry is dated.
- Entries vary in length.
- Standard spelling isn't always used.
- Journals may include sketches, illustrations, quotations, and so on.

Choose an Idea

- Keep a personal journal for a month. If you enjoy it, keep writing!
- Write a few journal entries from the point of view of a fictional or famous character. What kinds of things would this character record?
- Keep a nature journal. Use it to note the flowers and wildlife you find. Include sketches and reflections on what you see.
- Start a family journal at home. Invite your family members to write in the journal as often as they wish. Take the time to comment on and respond to each other's entries.
- Try an art journal. You might include information or articles about artists you admire, and try out some of the new techniques you've heard about.
- When you go on vacation with your family, keep a vacation or travel journal. Sketch the places you visit, glue in dried flowers or leaves from that place, add menus of special meals you had there, and so on.

Writing a Journal
Planning

1. Talk to friends and family members about whether they keep journals. What types of things do they write about?
2. Decide how you will keep your journal. Will you use a cassette, videotape, notebook, or computer?
3. Choose a special time and place to write. Try to set aside a regular time when you know you won't be interrupted.

Check These Out!

Read a variety of journals to get ideas for writing your own. Have you read any of these?
- *Zlata's Diary: A Child's Life in Sarajevo* by Zlata Filipovic
- *We Are Witnesses: Diaries of Five Teenagers Who Died in the Holocaust* by Jacob Boas
- *Eleanora's Diary: Journals of a Canadian Pioneer Girl* by Caroline Parry
- *In the Company of Whales* by Alexandra Morton

Drafting

FOR MORE ABOUT THE WORDS IN BOLD, SEE THE STYLE FILE.

1. Think about all of the things that are going on in your life. Choose one event, feeling, or idea to focus on and free write about it in your journal. Include everything you're thinking about. If you can't think of anything to write, start by writing that.
2. Write as little or as much as you want to each day. Your entries may become longer as you get used to writing in your journal. Remember to date all of your entries.
3. Take time to reflect and really think about your experiences as you write. Ask yourself questions such as How do I feel about what happened? or What have I learned? or What will I do next time?
4. Take some risks with sentence styles and punctuation. This is a place where you can experiment with language, words, ideas, and **tone** to develop your own **voice** as a writer. (See the Skill Focus on voice.)
5. You might want to include newspaper clippings, quotations, captions, cartoons, or photographs. Consider using illustrations, calligraphy, or sketches in your journal.

Revising

Consider these suggestions.

- Does your writing make sense?
- Have you included interesting details about the incidents or ideas you are writing about?
- Did you say everything you wanted to say?
- Have you taken the time to reflect on your experiences?
- Did you use interesting and accurate words to give details?
- Did you experiment with various sentence lengths and types and with punctuation?
- If you are writing from the point of view of a character, have you used the proper writing voice and point of view? Do you sound like that character?
- Did you include some sketches, pictures, or other visuals to make the journal pages look interesting?

Skill Focus

As a writer, your **voice** is the way you put your thoughts into words. Your voice is a combination of the language and words you use, the way you develop and express your sentences, the details you choose to include, and the tone you tell it in.

The tone you write in reflects your feelings about what you're writing. You might express anger, excitement, humour, sadness, wonder, or all of these!

Remember, when you write in a journal, you're writing for yourself. You can say whatever you want and you can express it any way you like!

For more about voice and tone, see page 152 of the Style File.

INFO !!

If you have decided to keep a personal journal and you don't want to share it, you don't need to revise or edit your writing. If you think you would like to share some or all of your journal, consider the suggestions for revising and editing.

Editing

FOR MORE ABOUT THE WORDS IN BOLD, SEE THE TOOL KIT.

Check your writing for

- correct **spelling**, especially of proper names
- **sentence variety**
- proper **punctuation**

Publishing

- Share your nature or art journals with a friend or group of friends, if you are comfortable doing so.
- If you are writing journal entries for a fictional or famous character, read your entries out loud using the character's voice and mannerisms.
- Publish your fictional journal entries by making them look like ancient documents, or by illustrating them with graphics or pictures appropriate to the writing ideas contained in the entries.
- Review your family journal occasionally with family members. Are there any comments or suggestions that you would like to discuss together?
- If you have asked questions or written about discoveries in your journal, you might talk to people about where you could find more information, or conduct some research by logging on to the Internet or visiting your local library.

Reflecting

- Who or what was helpful in getting you started on your journal?
- What did you learn about yourself from writing a journal?
- How might you incorporate ideas from your journal in your next narrative or essay?
- Why do you suppose we depend on journal entries to learn about history?

Narrative

- *Mysteries*
- *Fantasy Stories*
- *Pourquoi Tales*

Fast-paced action, mystery, excitement, out-of-this-world adventure—is this what you've been looking for? Have you given up finding it? Don't stop looking. It's all as close as the nearest bookshelf, in the world of narrative fiction.

Imagine the possibilities! Narrative allows you to go anywhere, do anything, and become anyone you want to be. You can travel to distant lands, go back (or forward) in time, solve age-old questions, and unravel new mysteries.

When you write narrative, you have the power to entertain and explain a variety of situations to your audience. Your imagination and the boundaries of believability are the only limits to the possible plots, settings, and characters that you can create.

Mysteries

Mystery stories entertain and challenge you at the same time. In order to figure out "who done it?" you need to think logically, and notice details. You feel good when you solve the mystery, so it's no wonder that mysteries are one of the most popular forms of narrative.

Many famous mystery stories and series have been transferred to TV and film, so even if you haven't read many mystery stories you may be familiar with such famous detectives as Sherlock Holmes, created by Sir Arthur Conan Doyle, and Miss Marple, created by Agatha Christie.

Learning how to write a good mystery takes practice, but it's exciting to watch others try to solve the puzzle you've created. You can build on skills you've already developed for writing narrative, such as creating a logical plot, interesting characters, and a believable setting; and add techniques specific to mysteries, such as setting up a puzzle, creating suspense, and planting clues.

Writing Goals

As you develop your mystery, ensure that you

- identify and model the features of mystery stories
- develop and organize plot ideas, characters, and clues
- plan and sequence events so the solution isn't revealed too early
- use writing techniques such as foreshadowing and suspense

Set one or two additional writing goals (skills you want to work on) for yourself.

Examine this excerpt of a mystery written by Nicole.

the mystery is set up early on

characters are quickly introduced

third-person point of view

dialogue is enclosed in quotation marks

sentences are well constructed and contain active verbs

clues are planted throughout the story

Nowhere to Run

It was ten after eight when Becky's friends arrived at her house. They parked their cars and walked, laughing and talking, up to the front door. They saw that the door was open slightly, and all the lights were out. Luke rang the doorbell, and when no one came to answer, they opened the door and entered the house.

"Becky?" Lisa called out. "Becky? Where are you?"

"Hello?" Mike called. "Anyone home?"

"Guys," Bobbi said softly, "something's wrong. I have a bad feeling about this."

Someone reached over and flicked on a light switch. The entrance was bathed in light, and they saw one of Rebecca's shoes on the floor. The heel was broken, as if she had fallen in them and it had snapped. The group ventured over to the broken shoe and saw another shoe halfway down a flight of stairs. At the bottom of these stairs they saw...

"Becky!" Bobbi cried. She ran down the stairs to her best friend. "No!" she sobbed. "No, Becky! No!" Bobbi cradled Rebecca's head in her arms and continued to cry.

Lisa screamed when she eyed Becky lying there on the floor, then hurried to join Bobbi.

"Someone call 9-1-1!" Luke shouted, also crowding around the body.

Rachel started toward the telephone, then stopped and looked back at Becky. She felt as if she were missing something important. Rachel noticed a streak of purple on Rebecca's hand. She recognized the colour right away.

MYSTERIES

Check These Out!

Reading mystery stories and novels will help you understand how to write one.
- *Vancouver Nightmare* by Eric Wilson (one of a series)
- *A Candidate for Murder* by Joan Lowery Nixon (one of a series)
- *False Face* by Welwyn Wilton Katz

INFO

Spy novels have many of the same features as mysteries. They involve a crime to be solved—usually espionage—and contain danger, suspense, and unexpected action. The main characters, usually spies or secret agents, also have special qualities that help to solve problems. Ian Fleming's James Bond is one popular example.

Features of Mysteries

- There is a mystery, a puzzle, or a crime to solve.
- The plot is believable—it could have happened.
- There is suspense, excitement, and unexpected action.
- The main character is usually a detective, either an amateur or a professional, who has a talent for finding clues and solving mysteries.
- There are often a number of secondary characters, including suspects (characters with a reason to commit the crime).
- Facts and clues are revealed throughout the story. Some clues may be false clues (called "red herrings") to keep the reader guessing.
- The story can be told from the third-person point of view of a narrator who is looking in on the action, or it can be told from the first-person point of view of the detective or the detective's helper.

Choose an Idea

- Choose a famous detective character you're familiar with and write a mystery using that character.
- Turn a real-life experience you've had, or have heard of, into a mystery.
- Take the plot of a mystery you've seen on television or at the movies and turn it into a story.
- Rewrite a mystery story that you've read and change the ending or the central character.

Writing a Mystery

Planning

FOR MORE ABOUT THE WORDS IN BOLD, SEE THE STYLE FILE.

1 Consider the **setting** for your mystery. Where and when will it take place? Describe your setting in detail. Give enough information that your reader will be able to see, hear, and smell it.

2 What is the **conflict** or problem that must be solved in your story? Was an important item stolen? Or does a kidnapper need to be caught?

3. Develop your main **character** using a character web. Consider the character's age, physical features, habits, personality, and any special talents. (For more about webs, see page 10.)
4. Then develop the secondary characters. Decide what relationship these characters have with one another and to the victim, if there is one. Establish a motive for each suspect. Give some of the suspects alibis and leave others unaccounted for at the time of the crime.
5. Write a rough outline to help you narrow the focus of your mystery and establish the **plot.** Think about what crime will be committed, by whom, where, why (the motive), and how it will be resolved.

Drafting

FOR MORE ABOUT THE WORDS IN BOLD, SEE THE STYLE FILE.

1. Decide who will tell the story. The **point of view** might be in the first person (told by a character), or in the third person (told by a **narrator**).
2. Determine what actions will take place after the crime and how your detective will solve the mystery. Include some unexpected action.
3. Decide how the clues will be revealed to the audience. Try not to give away too much information too early—don't give away the solution.
4. Use **dialogue** to move the plot along and to develop the characters.
5. Create **suspense** through the use of **foreshadowing.** (See the Skill Focus.)
6. Use a variety of sentence types—questions, commands, statements, exclamations—and vary the lengths of the sentences to add interest to your writing. (See the Skill Focus on correcting run-on sentences on page 32.)

Revising

Once you have a draft of your mystery, ask someone to review it to see that it makes sense, and that it's not too easy to figure out.
- Is the plot believable—could it have happened? Is the setting realistic?
- Is the mystery or puzzle set up early on in the story? Are the clues then revealed one at time?

INFO

Alibis are an important part of mystery stories. If a suspect has an alibi, that means this person can prove where he or she was when a crime was committed.

Skill Focus

Suspense is created by making the reader uncertain about what's going to happen in the story. **Foreshadowing**—suggesting what may happen in the future—builds suspense. It can be used to hint of possible danger, or to set up expectations. Words such as "maybe," "perhaps," and "possibly" can signal foreshadowing.

For more about foreshadowing and suspense, see pages 139 and 151 of the Style File.

Skill Focus

Watch out for **run-on sentences** in your writing. A run-on sentence occurs when two separate, complete ideas are joined with only a comma or are run together with no punctuation at all. To fix a run-on sentence, you could add a period and make them two separate sentences, or add a semicolon, or add a comma and a connecting word, such as "and," "but," or "then."

For more about sentences, see pages 167–171 of the Tool Kit.

- Have you included some false clues as well as real ones so the mystery isn't too easy to figure out?
- Are there some twists in the events and some unexpected action to keep the reader interested?
- Have you used interesting and informative words? Use a thesaurus to find alternatives to the word "said" in your dialogue; for example, "gasped," "shouted," "whispered."
- Did you vary the types and lengths of sentences?

Editing

FOR MORE ABOUT THE WORDS IN BOLD, SEE THE TOOL KIT.

Check your writing for

- **quotation marks** around dialogue
- complete **sentences** containing a **noun** and a **verb**
- correct **spelling**

Publishing

- Organize a mystery night for family members and read your story.
- Enter a mystery-writing contest or send your mystery to a magazine or newspaper that accepts students' writing.
- Make a computer printout of your story and circulate it, asking each reader to write a brief comment on what he or she likes about the story.
- Read your story aloud to classmates. Pause partway through and invite your audience to predict how the story will end.

Reflecting

- What new writing techniques did you develop by writing a mystery?
- What did you find the most challenging about writing a mystery?
- What suggestions would you offer to other students who are about to begin writing a mystery?

Fantasy Stories

Fantasy stories open the door to the vast worlds of our imagination. They usually feature people, objects, and events not found in the real world. Fantasy deals with alternate realities where scientific explanations and natural laws do not hold. What makes this type of story successful, however, is its ability to convince the audience to believe that it is possible.

Well-constructed plots, believable characters, vivid settings, and recognizable themes combine to form effective fantasy stories.

These stories can be lighthearted and appealing, such as *Mary Poppins* or *Peter Pan*, or they can deal with the universal themes of good versus evil, the strength and courage of the individual, or the search for truth.

Fantasy writing gives you the freedom to imagine, to create, and to entertain. So dare to go beyond the ordinary and let your imagination create a fantasy that will entertain your reader as well as yourself.

Writing Goals

As you develop your fantasy, ensure that you

- identify and model the features of fantasy stories
- use your imagination to develop a logical, entertaining plot
- create believable characters and action through dialogue and description
- use appropriate paragraph structure

Set one or two additional writing goals (skills you want to work on) for yourself.

Here is the opening for a fantasy story written by Emilio.

The Voyage There

In other circumstances the ride might have been enjoyable, but the seats of the coach felt hard to Jade's muscular back, and the snorting of the silky palomino horses hauling the coach sounded like rough growls to his pointy ears. The beautiful green forest of mighty Mallyrn trees passed by unnoticed. Jade knew something was wrong, but he couldn't put his finger on it.

The others in the carriage seemed unconcerned, except for a few grumbles about the bumpy road. Next to Jade was an ancient human with long silver hair who gently plucked her harp, filling the air with a gentle melody. Across from him, a young elfin maiden, barely 80 summers, listened intently to the music. Beside her young ward, the elf's guardian stared at the musician with untrusting eyes as the blue stone on her brow glowed softly in the dim light.

Not a word had been spoken by the passengers since the group had left Hoanere, and Jade quickly went over what he knew about them. The ancient musician was from far-off Phlann and was skilled in the use of music as charming magic. The young elf was the granddaughter of the mighty Celeborn, King of the Elves. The young one's guardian was well-trusted among the elves. Indeed, as a child Jade had been told stories of her mighty power over the element of air.

With such powerful spell casters on this trip, Jade doubted they would be challenged, but anxiety still gnawed at him.

Suddenly, shouts and war cries shattered his thoughts, and arrows pounded against the sides of the coach. The attackers charged straight for the coach. The elfin-bred steeds and knights in their heavy armour were no match for the mercenaries on foot, and the fight was quickly over.

The door of the coach swung open violently, and was wrenched from its hinges. A grizzled mercenary stood in the doorway with his blade drawn.

"Out," he said simply, in a rough voice.

The occupants of the carriage tumbled out. All of them were searched, and Jade's beloved magical dagger was taken from him.

"What's the meaning of this?" he demanded, only to be struck across the face.

Before him stood a motley crew of mercenaries with weapons drawn, ready to deal with any possible threat. The knights were tied up like trussed turkeys. The heavy-set horses snorted in terror as they pulled frantically at the disabled coach.

"They really scraped the bottom of the barrel to get these ruffians," the human bard remarked in a surprisingly young voice.

Jade eyed the mercenaries closely, and his photographic elfin memory recorded every detail. The leader of the band was very short, so short as to possibly be a gnome, but more portly and heavy set. Jade assumed that he was a dwarf. The others in the band were primarily humans dressed in mismatched armour from the scummiest taverns and slums across Terra.

One mercenary mounted, which surprised Jade, for this mob had obviously come from a black velvet mantle and wore a helmet. He was obviously a mage.

Features of Fantasy Stories

- A fantasy story
  - is believable within the framework of the story
  - is based on a theme (such as the struggle between good and evil; the loss of freedom; exploring a new world or an alternate way of life; love overcoming hate; or the search for truth)
  - may have an unpredictable ending—an element of surprise that leaves the reader thinking about the theme
- The characters
  - may be real people, fantastic characters (such as gnomes, elves, or talking animals), or creatures you create
  - often have special powers
- The setting is often in a world unknown to the reader that is very different from our own.
- The plot is original and creative. It may involve a quest or a special task to perform, imaginary kingdoms, magical happenings, or supernatural events.

Check These Out!

Read some fantasy stories to get ideas for writing your own. Have you read any of these?
- *The Giver* by Lois Lowry
- *Howl's Moving Castle* by Diana Wynne Jones
- *The Hunter's Moon* by O.R. Melling
- *An Acceptable Time* by Madeline L'Engle
- *The Hobbit* by J.R.R. Tolkien
- *Alice in Wonderland* by Lewis Carroll

Choose an Idea

- Write a fantasy story using the main character from a fantasy story you've read.
- Turn part of a strange dream into a believable fantasy story.
- Write a sequel to a fantasy story you've read and enjoyed.
- Imagine another world or a world within our own. Write a story using this world as the setting.
- Think of a fantastic or an unusual character—perhaps a talking animal, such as a unicorn or a dragon, or a creature you invent—and write a story about it.

Writing a Fantasy Story

Planning

FOR MORE ABOUT THE WORDS IN BOLD, SEE THE STYLE FILE.

1. Decide what you want to write about. Is there a particular **theme** you would like to explore? Jot down a few ideas and choose the best one.
2. Decide on your audience and consider how it will affect the way you write your story.
3. Decide on the **setting** (the time and place your story happens). It could be our world or a fantastic setting such as an imaginary land deep beneath the ocean. Jot down details about your setting.
4. What problem or **conflict** will your characters face or overcome? Will your main character be trapped in another time, or must she or he use a special power to save the world?
5. Develop your **characters** using a web. (See page 10 for more about webs.) Give your character traits that will enable him or her to solve the problem.
   - Is the character human, or an animal or object that behaves like a human? This is called **personification.** (See the Skill Focus.)
   - Does the character have any special powers?
   - Consider the character's look, age, habits, personality, and talents.
6. Decide what relationship the minor characters will have to the main character. Are they friends, strangers, or enemies?

Skill Focus

Personification is the giving of human qualities to an animal, object, or concept. For example, if one of your characters is a doll or stuffed animal, giving it a human personality would make it more interesting. Your audience will relate better to such a character if they know its feelings and thoughts.

For more about personification, see page 144 of the Style File.

Drafting

FOR MORE ABOUT THE WORDS IN BOLD, SEE THE STYLE FILE.

1. Using your ideas for the setting and conflict, and your character web as a guide, plan the action and write the events of your story.
   - Decide on the details of each event that will enhance your **plot** line and build to the **climax** and **resolution** of your story.
     – The opening should lead to the main problem.

NARRATIVE

- In the middle, show how the characters go about solving the problem.
  - Decide how the pieces of the story come together. End your story when the problem is solved.
- If magical "laws" have been established, they must remain consistent throughout the story. For example, a character can't suddenly develop new powers halfway through the story.

2 To make your fantasy story believable you can
  - describe your setting vividly to make your audience see and feel what the characters do
  - have your characters openly accept the fantasy happening around them
  - add real or imagined documents, such as maps, letters, pictures, or scrolls. (Use appropriate language to add believability; for example, use old-fashioned words for ancient scrolls.)

3 Write your story using description and **dialogue** to reveal the characters' personalities and to move the plot along.

Revising

Work with a classmate to revise your fantasy. Consider these suggestions.

- Have you created a believable setting, plot, and cast of characters?
- Will the theme be clear to the reader?
- Have you included fantasy elements, such as magical powers or talking animals, in your story?
- Is the magical power, unusual occurrence, or superpower you have created consistent throughout the story?
- Do the events occur in a logical order?
- Have you used dialogue to reveal the characters' personalities and to move the plot along?
- Did you use the best possible words, including descriptive adjectives and colourful, active verbs?
- Have you used proper paragraph structure? Is each paragraph a complete idea? (See the Skill Focus on paragraphs.)

Skill Focus

Look for natural breaks in your writing to insert **paragraphs**. You usually begin a new paragraph when introducing

1 a new person
2 a new place
3 a change of time
4 a change of speaker (in dialogue)
5 a change of idea

Remember to indent the first line of each new paragraph or leave a blank line between paragraphs.

For more about paragraphs, see pages 171–174 of the Tool Kit.

Editing

FOR MORE ABOUT THE WORDS IN BOLD, SEE THE TOOL KIT.

Check your writing for

- descriptive **adjectives** and **adverbs;** and colourful, active **verbs**
- a variety of **sentence** lengths and styles
- proper **punctuation,** especially **quotation marks** around dialogue
- correct **spelling**

Publishing

COMPUTER LINK

Formatting the short stories on computer using the same typeface and margins creates a consistent look for your class collection.

- Publish a class collection of short fantasy stories with your classmates. Donate it to your school library.
- Read your fantasy story to an audience of younger students or to another class.
- Illustrate your fantasy story and take it home to share with your family.
- Tape-record a dramatic reading of your story and add special effects if they are appropriate.

Reflecting

- What new writing techniques did you learn?
- What was interesting or challenging about writing fantasy?
- What suggestions would you give a classmate about writing a fantasy?

Pourquoi Tales

A pourquoi tale, or "why" tale, is a traditional type of narrative that has its origins in the distant past, when there was no written language. Stories would be passed down through the generations by word of mouth. As the stories were told and retold, they often changed a little to suit the style of the storyteller.

Pourquoi tales were told as a form of entertainment; they might explain things in nature, or give meaning to customs or traditions whose origins had been forgotten. The tales explain behaviour or characteristics of animals, such as why camels have humps; natural phenomena, such as land formations or why the sun rises in the morning and sets at night; and how certain customs developed.

The characters in pourquoi tales are often animals with human characteristics, such as the ability to speak, and gods that are responsible for delivering punishment or rewards.

Writing Goals

As you develop your pourquoi tale, ensure that you

- identify and model the features of pourquoi tales
- develop a simple and logical plot
- use description and dialogue to show action and emotion
- apply proper punctuation in dialogue

Set one or two additional writing goals (skills you want to work on) for yourself.

Read this pourquoi tale by Melissa.

How the Turtle Got Its Shell

Many years ago turtles were one of the fastest creatures on land. There was a particular turtle whom the natives liked to call Shelly. They often watched Shelly talking with her friends and laughing.

One day while Shelly was playing hide-and-seek with her friends, she hid inside a rock that had a small cave dug out of it.

"Help!" she screamed. "I'm stuck!" Everyone rushed to get Shelly out of the rock.

"Ha, ha," she laughed. "I was never stuck. I tricked you!"

All the animals groaned. "That was not funny. You better be careful because one day you might really get stuck."

"I'll never get stuck; I'm the swiftest animal on this land," boasted Shelly.

"She is too conceited and one day she will be in big trouble," thought her friends.

The next day when Shelly was playing with her friends, they decided to finish their game of hide-and-seek from the day before. Shelly decided that she would hide in the same rock. But this time when she tried to get out, she couldn't. She was stuck.

"Oh, no. What am I going to do? I can't get out! Help!" she cried. "I'm stuck!"

All of her friends heard her but no one believed her. Everyone thought she was just trying to trick them again. The day was very hot and as it got later, the wet mud that covered the inside of the rock dried and hardened. No matter how hard she tried, Shelly could not get out.

"Oh, well. I guess I'll have to walk home with this rock on my back," she finally decided.

She was not used to the heavy object on her back and she could no longer run swiftly. She couldn't even walk very fast.

When she got home she begged everyone to help her.

"I'm sorry, Shelly. It's too late. The mud has already dried up," her mother told her sadly.

"Now you know that it isn't good to play tricks on everybody," her father scolded. "I'm sorry, but your mother is right. You can't get out."

From then on, the rock on Shelly's back was known as a shell, after her name. And ever since then, turtles have been born with shells on their backs.

40 NARRATIVE

Features of Pourquoi Tales

- A pourquoi tale
  - usually begins with "A long time ago," "Many years ago," or a similar phrase
  - ends with a summarizing statement, such as "and that is why..." or "to this day the..."
  - has a title that tells what the story explains, for example, *How Spider Got a Bald Head*
- The characters may include
  - animals that have human characteristics
  - a god that delivers punishment or rewards
  - objects that are personified (take on human characteristics), such as the sun, trees, and so on
  - people within a specific culture, such as a chief, mayor, or tribal council member
- The plot is simple and includes
  - an explanation of a natural phenomenon, why animals have particular traits, or how certain customs of a group of people came to be
  - a quick introduction
  - fast-paced action
  - a logical and brief conclusion

Check These Out!

Reading a variety of pourquoi tales can help you to write your own. Have you read any of these?

- *When the World Was Young: Creation and Pourquoi Tales* retold by Margaret Mayo
- *Tales the Elders Told* by Basil H. Johnston
- *Why Corn is Golden, Stories about Plants* adapted by Vivien Blackmore
- *Native American Animal Origin Stories* collected and retold by Gerald Hausman

Choose an Idea

- Write a pourquoi tale explaining why an animal has certain traits; for example, why rabbits have long ears.
- Write a humorous pourquoi tale based on something silly or interesting that needs to be explained; for example, an odd custom, such as why people wave their hands to say goodbye.
- Choose a pourquoi tale you know and rewrite it from a different character's point of view.
- Write a pourquoi tale to explain a natural phenomenon, such as the presence of a local land formation or why leaves change colour in the autumn.
- Read a pourquoi tale, then develop a new story explaining the same thing in a different way.

Writing a Pourquoi Tale

Planning

FOR MORE ABOUT THE WORDS IN BOLD, SEE THE STYLE FILE.

1 Brainstorm ideas for a "why" story with a few classmates and choose the best one.

2 Think about the **setting,** the **characters,** the problem they will face, their actions, and the consequences of these actions that result in something being a certain way today. Jot down your ideas.

3 If your tale is about animals or people, you might draw a sketch of your main character (the **protagonist**) and any minor characters. Around the sketch list their physical characteristics, habitats, personality traits, enemies, and friends. (For more about protagonists, see the Skill Focus.)

4 If you are writing about a natural phenomenon, you might list or chart its various aspects. For example, if your pourquoi tale is explaining earthquakes, you could consider the causes and results of an earthquake. Think about the **personification** of an earthquake—what would it look like? How would it behave? What would it sound like if it spoke?

Drafting

FOR MORE ABOUT THE WORDS IN BOLD, SEE THE STYLE FILE.

1 Plan the action and write the events of your story.
- Decide who will tell the story and what the **point of view** will be—first person or third person.
- Use your jot notes and sketches to fill in the details of your **plot.**
  - The introduction should present the **conflict** or problem, characters, and setting in a few sentences.
  - Write events that maintain a fast-paced flow of action and lead to the resolution of the conflict. (Time can pass quickly in a single sentence, such as "Turtle walked and walked until he came to the end of the earth.")
  - The conclusion should be logical and brief, ending with a summarizing statement, such as "And to this day, turtles hide within their shells when they are afraid."

Skill Focus

The main character of a story is called the **protagonist**. This character is important and must be believable and interesting to your readers. If the protagonist is not interesting, your audience may not care about what happens to him or her.

While the protagonist is the main character, she or he is not necessarily a traditional hero. Your audience doesn't have to like the protagonist, they just have to be intrigued enough to want to find out what happens to the character in the end.

For more about protagonists, see page 144 of the Style File.

2 Pourquoi tales don't have a lot of detail but you should include some description and **dialogue** to express action, to show emotion, and to make the tale more interesting and readable. (See the Skill Focus.)

Revising

Consider these suggestions as you revise your story.

- Ask a friend to read your tale. Is it entertaining?
- Have you included all the events? Were you clear and concise?
- Is your choice of words appropriate for the audience?
- Did you start with "A long time ago" or a similar phrase?
- Did you vary your sentence types and lengths?
- Have you included dialogue and description?
- Did your story end with "to this day…" or "that is why…"?

Editing

FOR MORE ABOUT THE WORDS IN BOLD, SEE THE TOOL KIT.

Check your writing for

- **sentence** variety
- appropriate **paragraph** style
- proper **punctuation** including **quotation marks** in dialogue
- correct **spelling**

Publishing

- Format your tale on computer and create an eye-catching border.
- Create a class collection of pourquoi stories. Ask your principal if you could sell it as a fund-raiser.
- Illustrate your story and post it on a classroom bulletin-board display.

Reflecting

- What new writing techniques did you try? Were they successful?
- What tips would you give to a friend about writing a pourquoi tale?
- How do pourquoi tales differ from other forms of narrative?

Skill Focus

Dialogue is written conversation. Use dialogue to help your audience understand your characters by showing what the characters are like, how they speak, and what they are thinking and feeling. Dialogue can also move the plot along by explaining what the characters have done and what they plan to do. For more about dialogue, see page 138 of the Style File.

For more about proper punctuation for dialogue, see page 179 of the Tool Kit.

Humour

• Jokes

Are you a comedian at heart? Do you dream of earning a living by making people laugh? Many comedians make such a living. Of course, some of us are happy just to remember the punch line of jokes!

You don't have to be a comedian to enjoy humour. Sharing jokes, puns, and riddles has been an important part of most of our lives since the first knock-knock joke we told (repeatedly) as a kid.

Writing your own funny stories and silly jokes can be a challenge, but it's also a lot of fun to experiment with words—their meanings and sounds—as well as language, punctuation, and maybe even illustrations.

Jokes

It's hard to pinpoint just what makes a joke funny. Jokes can involve exaggerations, a silly or unexpected situation, funny dialogue, or a play on words. Whichever type of joke you choose, it's a great way to entertain your friends and family, and to "jazz up" a poster, newsletter, or speech.

People enjoy hearing a joke because there is a laugh and a surprise at the end. Writing and telling a joke is a challenge in itself because you have to figure out a clever way to reveal the clues without giving away the punch line. It's also a great way to show off your language skills because many jokes depend on playing with the meanings of different words.

Of all the jokes that are sure to get a laugh, and perhaps even a few groans, puns and riddles are two of the most popular.

Writing Goals

As you develop your joke, ensure that you
- identify and model the features of jokes
- brainstorm situations, ideas, phrases, and words for jokes
- experiment with homophones and homographs
- check spelling if using homophones and homographs

Set one or two additional writing goals (skills you want to work on) for yourself.

Here are some jokes that Nathan wrote for the class newsletter.

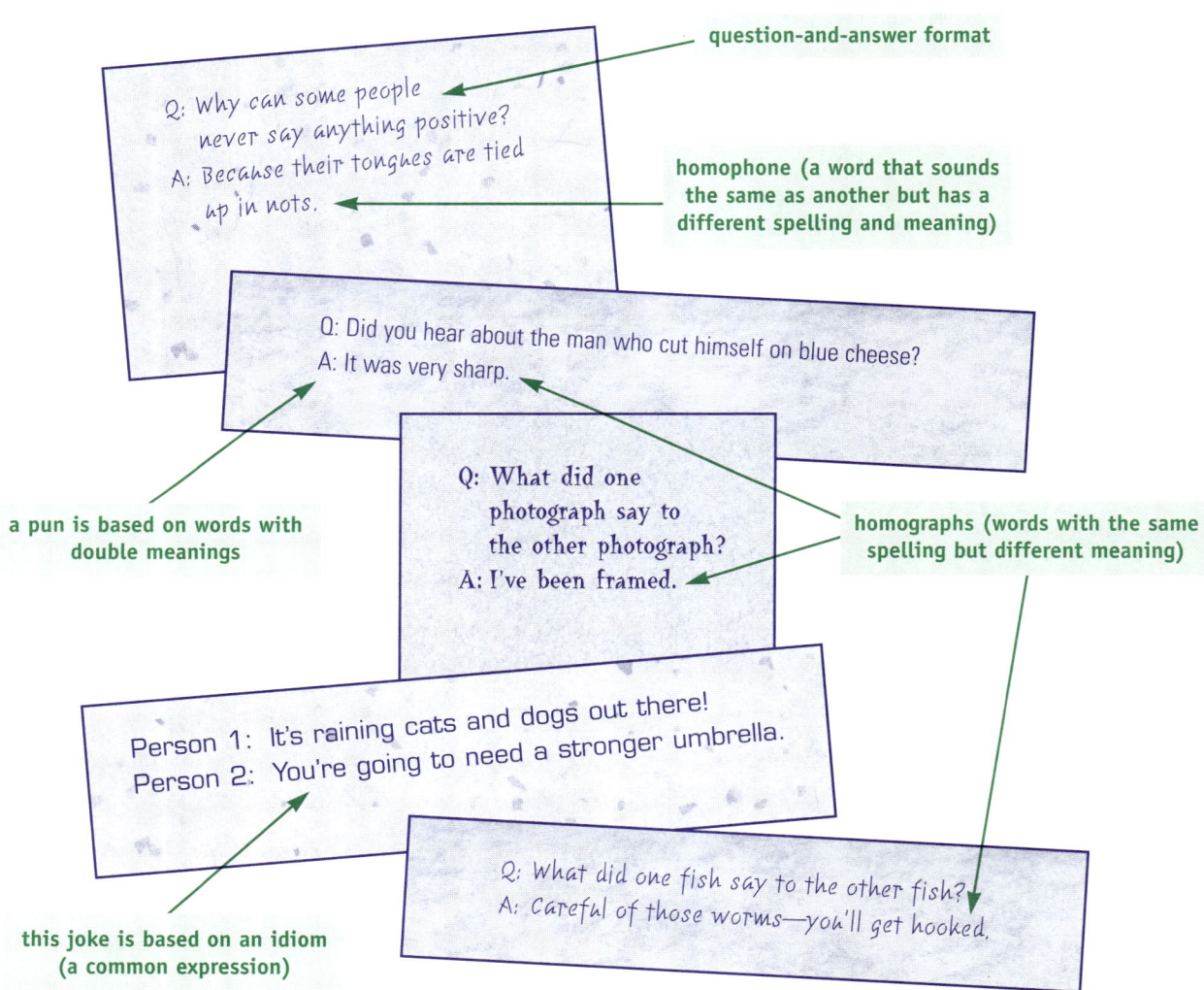

Q: Why can some people never say anything positive?
A: Because their tongues are tied up in nots.

— question-and-answer format
— homophone (a word that sounds the same as another but has a different spelling and meaning)

Q: Did you hear about the man who cut himself on blue cheese?
A: It was very sharp.

— a pun is based on words with double meanings

Q: What did one photograph say to the other photograph?
A: I've been framed.

— homographs (words with the same spelling but different meaning)

Person 1: It's raining cats and dogs out there!
Person 2: You're going to need a stronger umbrella.

— this joke is based on an idiom (a common expression)

Q: What did one fish say to the other fish?
A: Careful of those worms—you'll get hooked.

Features of Jokes

- The most common types of jokes are based on
  - homophones (sound-alike words such as "one" and "won")
  - almost sound-alike words such as "desert" and "dessert"
  - homographs (words with more than one meaning, such as "park—to park a car or to play in the park)
  - common or silly sayings

  Puns, for example, are based on words with double meanings or words that have similar sounds.
- Jokes use simple language.
- They are often written in question-and-answer form.

Choose an Idea

- Write a funny greeting card for a friend or relative. What kind of joke would be appropriate for a birthday card or a get-well card? Read some of the funny greeting cards in a card shop.
- Share some jokes in a letter or postcard to a friend or relative. Invite that person to send some jokes back to you.
- Send a friend an e-mail with your latest "puzzlin' pun."
- Create a comedy routine by yourself or with a few classmates. Write jokes your favourite comedian would tell. Videotape or audiotape your performance after you've practised it.
- Write some jokes to be read with the daily announcements—maybe about current or school events.

Check These Out!

Reading and telling jokes will help you understand how to write entertaining jokes of your own.
- *Funny You Should Ask: How to Make up Jokes and Riddles With Wordplay* by Marvin Terban
- *Side Splitters: Jokes and Riddles by Canadian Kids* collected and edited by Dennis McCloskey
- *Witcracks, Jokes and Jests from American Folklore* collected by Alvin Schwartz

Skill Focus

An **idiom** is a commonly used expression that means something different from what the words actually say. For example, the saying "it was raining cats and dogs" doesn't mean that cats and dogs were falling from the sky! Instead we understand it to mean that it was raining heavily.

The meaning that can be taken from what the words in an idiom actually say can often be used for humorous effect.

For more about idioms, see page 140 of the Style File.

Writing a Joke

Planning

FOR MORE ABOUT THE WORDS IN BOLD, SEE THE STYLE FILE.

1 Examine a variety of jokes to get an idea of what you think makes a joke funny.

2 Jot down any funny or silly ideas for use in your jokes. These might be funny things that have happened to you, things you've wondered about, "what if" situations, or common sayings (**idioms**) that you can play with. (See the Skill Focus for more on idioms.)

3 Brainstorm a list of sound-alike words (**homophones**), words that sound almost the same, and words with more than one meaning (**homographs**). Having a list of these words will help you write your jokes. Keep in mind that some jokes only work when you see them written down. (See the Skill Focus on homophones and homographs on page 49.)

Drafting

FOR MORE ABOUT THE WORD IN BOLD, SEE THE STYLE FILE.

1 Decide what type of joke you want to write. Will it be a question and answer? A section of funny **dialogue?**

2 Select a pair of words from your brainstormed list and write a sentence in which either word makes sense.

3 Now ask yourself questions about the sentence you've written. In what situation would it take place? Could it be a question or part of an answer to a question?

4 If the words you've chosen don't work out, choose another pair and try again.

Revising

Once you have a draft of your joke, ask someone to listen to it or read it. Consider the suggestions your editor makes as well as the following.

- Read your joke out loud. Does it make sense?
- Will other people find it funny?
- Have you used simple words and clear language?
- Have you used a play on words?
- Did you use the proper homophone for your meaning?
- Have you used an appropriate style, such as a question and answer or dialogue?

Editing

FOR MORE ABOUT THE WORDS IN BOLD, SEE THE TOOL KIT.

Check your writing for

- correct **spelling**
- proper **punctuation** and **capitalization**

Publishing

- Use your computer, or pen and ink, or coloured markers to write your jokes. Draw some illustrations or a cartoon to go along with them.
- Create your own joke book to share with your family and friends.
- Record your jokes on an audio cassette for others to enjoy.
- Begin a class joke book and invite classmates to add jokes they have written.
- Submit your jokes to your class or school newspaper.
- Have a class joke-a-thon. Share the jokes you and your friends have written.

Reflecting

- What new skills have you learned from writing jokes?
- What did you find most challenging about writing jokes?
- What do you think makes a joke good or bad?

Skill Focus

Homophones are words that sound alike but have different spellings and meanings. For example:

*When the rain falls, does it go up again? Sure, in **dew** time.*

plays on the meanings of "due" and "dew." A joke with homophones needs to be written down for the audience to be able to recognize the play on words.

Homographs are words that have the same spelling but different meanings. For example:

What makes the Tower of Pisa lean? It doesn't eat much.

Jokes with homographs are great for telling out loud because the audience can immediately recognize the pun.

For more about homophones and homographs, see pages 184–185 of the Tool Kit.

Research

- **Research Reports**
- **Surveys**
- **Profiles**

Information surrounds us and plays a part in almost all aspects of our lives. News shows on television and radio, articles in magazines and newspapers, Web sites on the Internet, flyers in our mailboxes, surveys at the supermarket, classroom reports—how many of these types of information reach you every day?

Should we accept this information as the truth? Should we believe everything we read? Certainly not! We want proof that this information has been researched and is based on sound arguments with supporting facts, details, and examples.

The same holds true when you write to report information and share facts. The audience wants to know that you have done your research thoroughly and that you are reporting in a thoughtful manner. So dig deep, get all the facts, and be creative in your presentation!

Research Reports

In most subject areas, you are asked to do research and to report your information or findings to your classmates or others. Research reports are a great way for you to show off what you've learned and to share this information with others who are interested.

Reports are different from other writing formats because they require the collecting, analysing, and presenting of information. The challenge is to get the scoop on fresh information and to present it clearly, concisely, and in an engaging manner.

Writing Goals

As you develop your research report, ensure that you
- identify and model the features of research reports
- develop and use key questions to help focus your research
- organize and present the information in an interesting way using headings and subheadings
- use standard grammar, punctuation, and spelling

Set one or two additional writing goals (skills you want to work on) for yourself.

Take a look at this report about copper that Erin wrote for her science class.

Where Would We Be Without Copper?

Have you ever noticed the greenish roofs of many older buildings, such as the Parliament Buildings in Ottawa? Would you believe that these roofs are actually made of the same metal as the reddish-orange coloured kettles you've seen? Both of these items, and many more important aspects of our lives, are made of, or depend on, copper. Copper is a soft but tough metal that has been used by humans for more than five thousand years. This report will explain why copper is the most useful metal we have.

(the introduction sets the focus for the report)

The History of Copper

Copper was one of the first metals to be used by people. Early Neolithic peoples of the late Stone Age used copper in its natural metallic form instead of stone. When metallurgy (the science of working with metals) became popular in Egypt, copper was alloyed (a metal mixed with another metal or non-metal) with tin to become bronze.

Bronze became the most popular metal for making weapons, tools, and jewellery because it was very hard. Many different peoples, including the Chinese, the Incas in Peru, and American Indians, used bronze. This period of time is known as the Bronze Age. The Bronze Age passed into the Iron Age, not because iron was a harder or better metal than bronze, but because it was easier to find.

(headings are used to organize information)
(technical terminology may be included)
(explanatory paragraphs containing topic sentences and supporting details are used)

Uses of Copper Today

Today copper is used for much more than roofs and kettles. Copper conducts heat and electricity better than any metal except silver. Half of the copper produced in Canada is used for electrical and telecommunications wire and cable (in telephones, radios, and televisions) and electric motors.

Copper can be mixed with substances other than bronze to make new copper alloys. Combined with zinc, copper forms brass, and when copper is combined with nickel, nickel silver is made. (There is no actual silver in nickel silver.) Copper alloys are used to make industrial machinery, refrigerators and vacuum cleaners, turbines, locomotives, and plumbing pipes. Nearly all coins contain copper.

Copper has been a very important metal throughout history. It is also important to many aspects of our lives today including tools, appliances, communication, transportation, money, and industry. What would life be like without copper?

(uses an objective style based on facts, and a formal tone)
(the conclusion summarizes the main points)

Features of Research Reports

- Research reports
  - present researched information in an organized manner
  - use precise, descriptive language and may include technical terminology related to the subject
  - are usually written in an objective style (based on the facts, not your point of view) and in a formal tone
  - have an introduction that sets the focus for the report
  - are usually written in paragraphs with the main idea of each paragraph expressed in a clear topic sentence
  - often categorize information using headings
  - end with a conclusion that summarizes the main points
  - may also include pictures, diagrams, and charts to emphasize specific points and to support the main ideas

Check These Out!

Examining different types of research reports can give you ideas for writing your own report. Ask your teacher, schoolmates, friends, and family if they have any research reports you could check out.

Choose an Idea

- Write a research report about a famous person whom you admire.
- Investigate an historical event and write a research report about it.
- Look through a newspaper or watch the news to find a current or "hot" issue (for example, a local environmental issue, or a new cancer treatment).
- Research a topic of interest to teenagers and write a report about what you discover.
- Write a research report about a topic you're studying in social studies, science, or art.

COMPUTER LINK

Conduct research using CD-ROMs and online computer searches. Many encyclopedias and indexes are on CD-ROM. Access the World Wide Web and check out the sites for more current information. Some information on the Web is updated every day. You can download any relevant information on your topic and print out a hard copy.

Writing a Research Report

Planning

1. List some topics you know about or want to know more about, then choose one that appeals to you.
2. Focus on the topic by developing a word web or by brainstorming different aspects of the subject you could research.

3. Narrow your topic. A topic that is too general will be difficult to research. Jot down a list of questions you would like to find the answers to.
4. Consider your audience. What do they need to know?
5. Locate sources of information about your topic.
   - Use your school and public libraries.
   - Find experts on your topic to write or talk to.
   - Ask teachers, friends, and family members what they know about the topic. (For more about conducting research, see pages 154–159 of the Tool Kit.)
6. Make clear, brief notes from your research. Write each question you want to answer on a separate recipe card and then, in your own words, record the information that answers each question. Always note the source at the top of the card in case you need to verify quotations or other information later on. (For more about note-taking, see page 154 of the Tool Kit.)

Drafting

FOR MORE ABOUT THE WORD IN BOLD, SEE THE STYLE FILE.

1. Write an outline for your report in point form. An outline is important for organizing your information. An outline is usually divided into three main parts.
   - Begin with an introduction, which states the purpose of the report and gives a little background. To get your reader's attention, use something interesting, such as a direct quotation, a description, or an unusual statement.
   - Follow this with the body of the report. Include three to six main sections developed from the categories you've researched.
   - End with a conclusion, which gives a summary of the information and emphasizes the purpose of the report.
2. Use these points to develop the paragraphs of your report. Each explanatory paragraph should have a main idea or topic sentence and then details that clearly support and develop the idea. (See the Skill Focus on explanatory paragraphs.)
3. Add main headings and subheadings if you think they would help the reader. Your headings could be in the form of questions.

Skill Focus

When writing your research report you will probably be using **explanatory paragraphs** to explain circumstances, experiences, or events. This type of paragraph answers the questions *who, what, where, when, why,* and *how* and helps to make a research report clear and accurate.

Explanatory paragraphs contain a clearly stated topic sentence somewhere (usually, but not always, at or near the beginning of the paragraph) and closely related sentences that support the topic sentence with detailed information.

For more about explanatory paragraphs, see page 174 of the Tool Kit.

> Introduction
> Main Idea   - copper plays an important role in our lives
> Background   - reddish-orange coloured metal
>   - soft but tough
>   - has been around for more than 5000 years
> Purpose   - to show that copper is the most useful metal
>
> Main Sections
> Section One - History of Copper
> 1. First Point - one of the first metals used by people
>   # 1 detail - used by Neolithic people (define?)
>   # 2 detail - metallurgy (define) began in Egypt where copper was alloyed
>   (define) with tin to make bronze
> 2. Second Point - copper was very important in the Bronze Age
>   # 1 detail - many different peoples used copper to make tools, weapons, and
>   jewellery
>   # 2 detail - bronze is harder than iron - Bronze Age passed to Iron Age only
>   because iron was easier to find
> Section Two - Uses of Copper Today
> 1. First Point - copper is used for much more than roofs and kettles
>   # 1 detail - copper conducts heat and electricity better than any metal except silver
>   # 2 detail - half of Cdn copper is used for electrical and telecommunications
>   wire and cable (telephones, radios, television) and electric motors
> 2. Second Point - copper can be alloyed with substances other than tin - alloyed
>   with zinc to make brass, and with nickel to make nickel silver (no silver in it)
>   # 1 detail - alloys used to make industrial machinery, refrigerators and vacuum
>   cleaners, turbines, locomotives, and plumbing pipes
>   # 2 detail - copper is part of nearly all coins
>
> Conclusion
> Copper is very important to many aspects of our lives today including tools, appliances, communication, transportation, money, and industry. What would life be like without copper?

4 Use precise, descriptive language and avoid **jargon** by defining any specialized terminology. (See the Skill Focus for more about avoiding jargon.)

5 Consider using direct quotations, tables, graphs, charts, or maps to support the points you're making and to make your report more interesting and easier to understand.

6 List the sources you used to write your report in a bibliography. (For more about bibliographies, see page 155 of the Tool Kit.)

Skill Focus

Jargon is specialized terminology that is used in certain occupations or situations. Unless your audience is familiar with this terminology, they won't understand its use.

Avoid jargon by substituting more common terms, or by defining or explaining any specialized terminology that can't be replaced.

For more about jargon, see page 142 of the Style File.

Revising

Work with a classmate and consider these points as you revise.

- Is the purpose of the report clear?
- Are all new points introduced in the body of the report?
- Is the main idea or topic sentence clear in each paragraph?
- Have you used supporting details?
- Do your paragraphs follow a logical sequence?
- Does the conclusion connect to the introduction?
- Have you read your report aloud to yourself or to a friend?
- Are there unnecessary words or sentences that could be removed?
- Have you defined any technical terminology?

Editing

FOR MORE ABOUT THE WORDS IN BOLD, SEE THE TOOL KIT.

Check your writing for

- correct **punctuation** (commas and quotation marks in direct quotations)
- consistent tense of **verbs**
- complete **sentences**
- well-organized **paragraphs**
- correct **spelling**

Publishing

- Present your research report to your class. Use visuals, slides, or overheads to help you.
- If you're researching a current newsworthy issue, send your research report to the local newspaper.
- Distribute copies of your report to schoolmates, parents, and teachers.

Reflecting

- What did you learn about conducting research?
- Why are research reports a good way to present information?
- Are there other areas of your research that you would like to explore?

Surveys

A survey is a useful way to collect and record information that can't be found anywhere else. This is because very often surveys collect current opinions and views from people and provide market-research information about the latest trends. For example, surveys can help you find out what people think about a certain issue, a service, a product, or perhaps what they think needs to be changed about the world. Surveys can also provide statistics to support an opinion or point of view.

Filling out a survey can be fun because we are flattered when other people want to know our opinions. We enjoy reading the results of surveys because we like to compare our opinions with those of others.

Think about how conducting a research survey could help you gather current information to support a topic you're writing about.

Writing Goals

As you develop your survey, ensure that you
- identify and model the features of surveys
- identify a target group for your survey
- write clear, concise questions (open-ended, yes/no, multiple choice)
- tabulate results and draw conclusions

Set one or two additional writing goals (skills you want to work on) for yourself.

Zoran created this survey to find out how much homework students do and how they feel about it.

Homework Survey

In this survey I want to discover how much homework is done by students in my school and if students feel it helps them in class.

1. What grade are you in? ____
2. Are you:
   Male ____ Female ____
3. Do you have homework almost every night?
   Yes ____ No ____
4. What is the average number of hours a night you spend doing homework? Please check one of the following:
   ____ 0 - 1
   ____ 1 - 2
   ____ 2 - 3
   ____ more than 3
5. What classes do you have homework in? Check all that apply.
   English ____   French ____
   Math ____   Social Studies ____
   Science ____   Other ____
6. How do you feel about how much homework you get?
   Do you think you get:
   ____ Too much homework
   ____ Enough homework
   ____ Not enough homework
7. When do you do your homework?
   ____ Right after school
   ____ After dinner
   ____ Before bed
   ____ Other
8. Do you do your homework:
   Alone ____ With a friend ____
9. Do you finish your homework?
   Always ____
   Sometimes ____
   Never ____
10. Do you think doing homework helps you to be a better student?
   _____
   _____

Annotations:
- the topic for investigation is clearly stated
- yes/no questions may be used
- may include multiple-choice questions
- a personal information section
- clear, concise questions
- open-ended questions can be answered in any way

Features of Surveys

- A survey is used to collect information.
- The topic for investigation is clearly stated in the title or in an introduction to the survey.
- Surveys usually include a personal information section asking for relevant information, such as the person's age, gender, education, occupation, and so on.
- A survey can be conducted through a written questionnaire (a list of questions), or the questions may be asked by someone and the answers recorded.
- Some questions may require a simple yes/no answer, others may be open-ended (answered in any way), or a choice of answers may be given (multiple choice).
- Results of surveys are usually analysed and reported on in a written report, an article, a graph, as a list of statistics, or in an oral report.

Choose an Idea

- Conduct a survey to find out about your schoolmates—their favourite hobbies or interests, how they spend their spare time, or their favourite subjects in school.
- Conduct a survey about your school. What kinds of things help you become better students? What kinds of changes need to be made to make your school better? Target different groups of people—students, teachers, school administrators, parents, custodians, and secretaries. Look for similarities and differences in the results of your surveys.
- Conduct a survey about your classmates' reading habits. What are their favourite books and who are their favourite authors?
- Conduct a survey to find out how people in your community feel about an issue that is important to you, your school, or to your community.
- Conduct a product survey to discover why people buy the product brands they do. For example, do they base their decision on habit, on advertising, word-of-mouth, price, or packaging? Predict the most popular reason and then conduct a survey to find out if you're right.

Check These Out!

Look for surveys in your favourite magazines and in newspapers. You might also examine
- the magazine *Consumer Reports*
- the Web site "The Daily" (www.statcan.ca) at Statistics Canada

INFO

A variety of question types will give you both general and specific information.
- **Multiple-choice questions** give you a choice of more than one answer.
- **Close-ended questions** are answered by a yes or no. Your question has to be very clear.
- **Open-ended questions** can be answered in any way. The answers will be more individual than with the other types of questions.

Writing a Survey

COMPUTER LINK

Design your questionnaire on computer, if possible. Leave a double space between the questions and include lines for the reader to write on. In multiple-choice questions, use boxes for the reader to check off. Organizing your survey in this way makes it easier to read and respond to.

Planning

1. Decide what you would like to investigate.
   - What do you hope to find out?
   - Think about how a survey could help to explain or clarify any information in your writing.
   - Brainstorm a list of possible questions for your survey.
2. Decide whom you will target in your survey—other students, teachers, parents, family members, or people in your community. Whom you survey will depend on what you're trying to find out. Some topics may require you to survey different groups of people.

Drafting

1. Develop a written questionnaire. Make sure that the questions are clear. If a person has to guess what you mean, the results won't be accurate. Also, be sure not to use any words that give a hint about what you think. This is called your "bias."
2. You will probably need to know something about the people you survey, such as their age, gender, occupation, and so on. Include a personal section on your survey for this kind of information.
3. You may also want to describe briefly what you are trying to achieve in your survey. This will help the participants to complete your survey.
4. Conduct your survey. Ask questions of people and record the answers, or photocopy your questionnaire and hand it out.
5. Once you've conducted your survey, tabulate the results by counting the number of people surveyed and finding out how many of those people answered in a certain way. Interpret the results and write down any conclusions you came to.

6 There are several ways to represent your results.
  - You could present your results as a series of statistics. Use numbers: for example, out of 100 students, 60 spend two to three hours a night doing homework; or out of 100 people, 47 suggested reducing the size of classes.
  - You might graph the most interesting points. For example, if you wanted to look at how much homework a student does, you could graph the average number of hours each of the different groups of people reported.

INFO

When the age, gender, income, or occupation of a group is taken into account, it is referred to as the "demographics" of a group. Using the demographics of a group is useful when you are trying to compare the results of one group with another. For example, the opinions about what makes a good student may differ between a group of students and their teachers or parents. Differences in the age and gender of the participants may also produce different results.

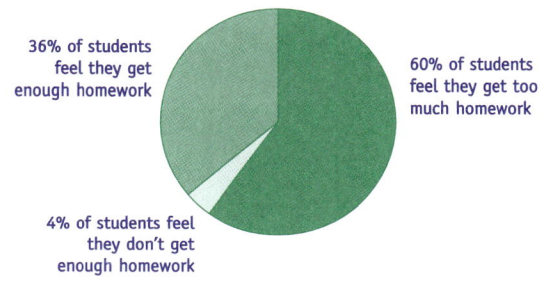

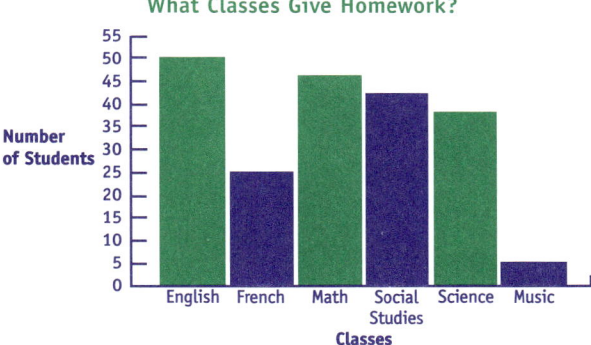

7 Write up your results as a report and add your explanation of the reason for the results. If you used open-ended questions, you could share some examples of the more interesting answers as quotations in a report.

SURVEYS

Skill Focus

When you are writing your results and conclusions, help your reader understand your points and statements by using **transitional expressions** to link your thoughts. For example, to compare two points or to add a point, use expressions such as "also," "as well," and "in addition." To add emphasis, use "especially" or "more importantly." When summarizing or concluding, use expressions such as "as a result," "therefore," or "finally."

For more about transitional expressions, see page 168 of the Tool Kit.

Revising

Once you have a draft of your survey, ask a classmate or adult to review it to see if it is easy to complete. Consider the following.

- Is the purpose for the questionnaire briefly stated?
- Are the questions clear? Will they provide the information you need?
- Have you read the questions out loud to listen for any errors?

Once you've analysed the results of your survey, share your report with classmates. Ask them to think about the following.

- Has your research question been answered?
- Are the results clearly described?
- Are any differences and similarities in viewpoints made clear and explained?

Editing

FOR MORE ABOUT THE WORDS IN BOLD, SEE THE TOOL KIT.

Check your writing for

- correct **spelling**, **grammar**, and **punctuation**
- enough space left between the questions

Publishing

- Share the results of your survey with the people who participated.
- Present your survey in an oral report, using graphs or statistics for overheads.
- Send the results of your survey about a community issue to a local newspaper with some suggestions of how the issue or situation might be improved as a result of what you learned.
- If you did a survey about the school, share your results in the school newspaper, or display them in the school library or resource centre.

Reflecting

- What surprised you most about the results of your survey?
- What would you do differently the next time you write a survey?

RESEARCH

Profiles

Profiles are short articles that offer information about interesting people, companies, organizations, and even places. They are usually published in newspapers and magazines. A profile puts the spotlight on a subject and tries to capture what makes it special.

Profiles can be about ordinary people who have experienced remarkable or extraordinary things in their lives, people who have unusual jobs or hobbies, or people who are viewed as heroes. Profiles are also written to highlight companies or organizations that have achieved success in specific areas. Travel articles are often profiles of unusual and interesting locations throughout the world.

People enjoy reading profiles because they like reading about the unusual or famous. As a writer, learning how to write a profile can help you discover new and interesting facts and information about a person, a group of people, or a place. Then it's up to you to select the facts and piece them together in a way that appeals to your audience.

Writing Goals

As you develop your profile, ensure that you

- identify and model the features of profiles
- conduct research to gather facts and information
- select main ideas and support them with details and facts
- use descriptive language and quotations to describe the subject

Set one or two additional writing goals (skills you want to work on) for yourself.

Here's a profile Jill wrote about her grandfather.

heading sums up what the profile is about

the opening paragraph states the main idea of the profile

formal and informative writing style

details and facts support the main idea

descriptive language is used

One Terrific Grandpa

Grandpa Wilson had a very tough life growing up and trying to make a living for his family during the Depression. During that period of time there were not a lot of jobs nor did people make much money. Even if you did have money, things like wool blankets and some foods were not available; therefore, my grandpa had to make a living for himself.

Grandpa became a great woodsman—cutting, splitting, and piling rods of wood for people in order to make money. Also, he would trap muskrats and raccoons for their fur so it could be sold to buyers for small amounts of money.

In the summer Grandpa spent many hours a day in the tobacco fields to make a living for his family. Also in the summer he would drive to the lake to get different kinds of fresh fish and put tubs of ice in the trunk of this car and peddle fresh fish to all the neighbours in the community. Back then Grandpa knew what hard work it was to make a living from day to day.

My grandpa supported my grandma and three children (one being my mom) giving them much love and support. Many years later my brother and I came into Grandpa's life, and that was to our advantage. We were spoiled rotten. It seemed every time he came to visit we couldn't get enough hugs and kisses, along with many special treats.

Listening to many wonderful stories about Grandpa and receiving that special loving attention has made Grandpa Wilson a very important and special person in my life. Unfortunately, Grandpa passed away on July 10th, 1994.

Features of Profiles

- A catchy headline helps direct the reader's attention to the profile and sums up what the profile is about in a few words.
- Profiles usually begin with an opening paragraph or "lead" that sets the tone of the article and states the main idea.
- Details and facts are added to support the main idea and to tell *who, what, where, when, why,* and *how.*
- A profile is organized into paragraphs.
- Headings may be used to organize the information.
- Descriptive words are carefully chosen to create a clear picture of the subject in the minds of the reader.
- Boxing, bold type, and shading are often used to highlight important information.
- The style of writing may be informal and entertaining or more formal and informative.
- Pictures often accompany a profile to provide more details and a clearer image of the subject.

Choose an Idea

- Choose a famous person from history and develop a profile about that person.
- Create a profile of a friend. Interview your friend's family as part of your research.
- Profile a teacher or student who has made a difference to your school or to life in your community.
- Write a profile about a place that is special to you—a park, a cottage, or a place you visited on vacation.
- Profile an organization that does good work in your community but may not be well known.

Check These Out!

Read a variety of profiles to get ideas for writing your own. Take a look at magazines for celebrity profiles and at newspapers for profiles of people and travel destinations. Examine books such as

- *Great Women in Sports* by Anne Janette Johnson
- *Rising Stars of the NBA* by Joe Layden
- *Lives of the Athletes— Thrills, Spills (and What the Neighbors Thought)* by Kathleen Krull

Writing a Profile

Planning

1 Decide on a subject for your profile. Remember that there has to be enough information available about your subject to write an interesting profile.

2 Think about what kind of information you want to include. Consider the details that make your subject special or different. Brainstorm a list of questions you would like to have answered.

3 Research your subject in magazines, newspapers, encyclopedias, reference books, or on the Internet. Television and radio shows are other possible sources of information. If possible, interview your subject, or interview other people who know the person well. (For more about conducting interviews, see page 159.) If your subject is a famous or historical person, you might find information in a biography or autobiography. Record some interesting quotations from these sources.

Drafting

FOR MORE ABOUT THE WORDS IN BOLD, SEE THE STYLE FILE.

1 Review your information and choose a focus or main idea for your profile. Create an outline for your profile by listing five or six statements that support the main idea. Select details and facts from your research to support each statement. These statements with the supporting details will form each of your paragraphs.

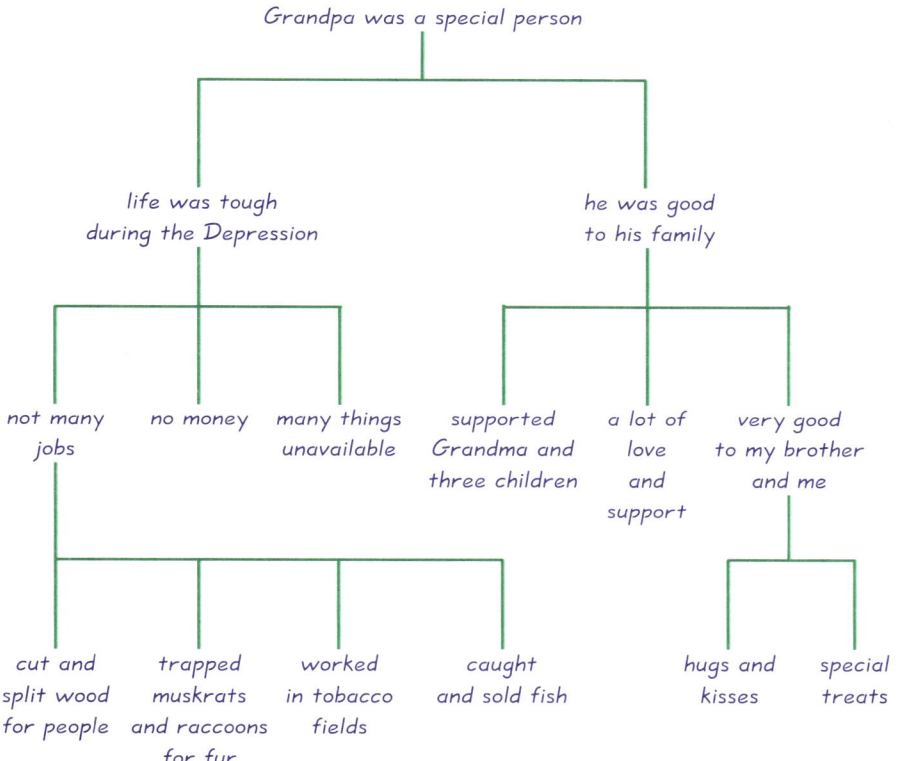

Skill Focus

Descriptive paragraphs describe a person, a place, a thought, or an idea. They make the reader see, hear, smell, taste, and feel what you're describing.

Use descriptive paragraphs to make your subject come alive for the reader.

For more about descriptive paragraphs, see page 172 of the Tool Kit.

Use **imagery** within your descriptive paragraphs to create pictures in the reader's mind. Imagery can also appeal to the senses of touch, taste, smell, and hearing. Use concrete descriptions that include specific nouns, descriptive adjectives and adverbs, and active verbs to create vivid images of your subject.

For more about imagery, see page 140 of the Style File.

2 Set the **tone** of your profile at the beginning and write an interesting **lead** that expresses your main idea. The lead should answer the questions *who, what, where, when, why, how,* and introduce your subject to the reader.

3 Balance the amount of factual information with descriptions of the place, person, or setting, and with quotations about the subject or by the person.

4 *Show* the readers your subject rather than tell them. Try to
- give detailed descriptions using descriptive paragraphs and **imagery** so the reader will have a clear picture of the person or place. Note the special details that make your subject different from others. (See the Skill Focus for more about descriptive paragraphs and imagery.)

Skill Focus

There are two ways to include **quotations** from your research or interviews:

1 direct quotations or
2 indirect quotations.

A **direct quotation** is a word-for-word report of what someone said, and it needs quotation marks.

An **indirect quotation** is a summary of a direct quotation and doesn't need quotation marks.

DIRECT QUOTATION
Flannery said, "The Red Cross was there to help me when no one else seemed to care."

INDIRECT QUOTATION
Flannery felt that the Red Cross was there to help him when no one else seemed to care.

For more about quotations and use of quotation marks, see page 179 of the Tool Kit.

- let your subject speak. Use quotations from your interview or other sources that express the person's character or personality. (For more about quotations, see the Skill Focus.)

5 Consider using headings to help organize your profile.

6 Wrap up your profile with a thoughtful summary or "snapshot" of the subject, or leave your audience with something to think about.

7 Write your headline last. The headline should sum up the profile in a few catchy words and attract your reader.

8 Use photographs cut from newspapers or magazines, or sketches or illustrations you've drawn to emphasize the points you're making. Each picture should have a caption (a sentence or phrase explaining it).

Revising

As you revise, consider the following suggestions.

- When you have completed a draft of your profile, read it aloud to yourself or to a friend. Does it make sense? Is it well organized?
- Do you have an interesting lead?
- Have you answered the questions *who, what, where, when, why,* and *how?*
- Are your statements supported with details and facts?
- Have you used description and quotations to bring the subject to life for your readers?
- Is the tone of the profile consistent throughout?
- Does the title capture the reader's attention and sum up the profile?
- Have you used visuals to enhance your story?
- Have you asked a classmate or an adult to give you some feedback? Consider the ideas and use any you like to make your writing better.

Editing

FOR MORE ABOUT THE WORDS IN BOLD, SEE THE TOOL KIT.

Check your writing for

- variety in your **sentence** constructions
- proper **paragraph** structure
- correct **capitalization** for **proper nouns** (names of people and places)

Publishing

- Publish the profile of your friend in the school newspaper or on a bulletin board.
- Create a bulletin-board display of class profiles for an Open House or Meet the Teacher Night.
- Publish your profile of a teacher or student in your school newspaper.
- Print your profile of a friend on the computer, add photographs or illustrations, and give it to your friend as a gift.
- Write your profile without naming the subject and invite classmates to guess who the subject is.
- Print a few copies of your profile and distribute them to classmates and family members.

Reflecting

- What new research or writing techniques did you learn as you wrote your profile?
- What characteristics or qualities did you come to admire in the person, place, or group you profiled?
- What is it about profiles that makes them different from other types of magazine or newspaper articles?

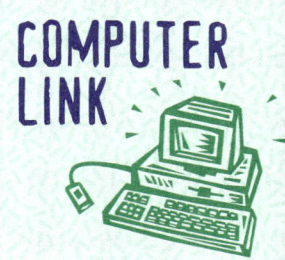

COMPUTER LINK

When formatting your profile, you might use a two-column design. It's often easier to read than one wide column and gives a professional look to newspaper or magazine pieces. (If your computer will only print one column, simply reduce the column's width to the appropriate size, print out the narrow column, then cut and paste the columns side by side on another sheet of paper. Add headlines and photocopy the result.)

MESSAGES

- **THANK-YOU NOTES**
- **FRIENDLY LETTERS**

When was the last time you shared some information with someone? When was the last time you did so without talking in person or on the phone? If you're like most people, it's probably been a while.

The computer is a wonderful machine for communicating—e-mail and chat rooms on the Web are great ways to share knowledge and opinions—but everyone still loves to get regular mail. Receiving a crazy letter from a long-lost friend or getting an invitation to a party can really make your day!

So why not make someone else's day? Write a funny, friendly letter to a friend or relative. You can include every single detail about your life and it'll only cost you the price of a stamp! Or write the thank-you note you've been telling yourself you should write. Let your friends and relatives know how much you appreciate them and what they've done for you.

Thank-You Notes

Writing a thank-you note is a thoughtful way of letting friends and relatives know that you appreciate something they've done for you. You can send a note to acknowledge someone's extra efforts, to give thanks for a gift you have received, or to thank someone for attending a special event.

You can make your thank-you note as special or individual as the person you are sending it to. Making a special effort to personalize your note and making it fun to read shows that you care.

Just think of all the nice things that people do for you, for your family, or for your friends. Wouldn't it be great to express your gratitude with a sincere thank-you note?

Writing Goals

As you develop your thank-you note, ensure that you

- identify and model the features of thank-you notes
- develop a tone that is appropriate for your audience and purpose
- write a brief message stating what you are thankful for
- identify and use informal language, such as abbreviations and contractions

Set one or two additional writing goals (skills you want to work on) for yourself.

Caitlyn sent this note to thank a friend for a gift.

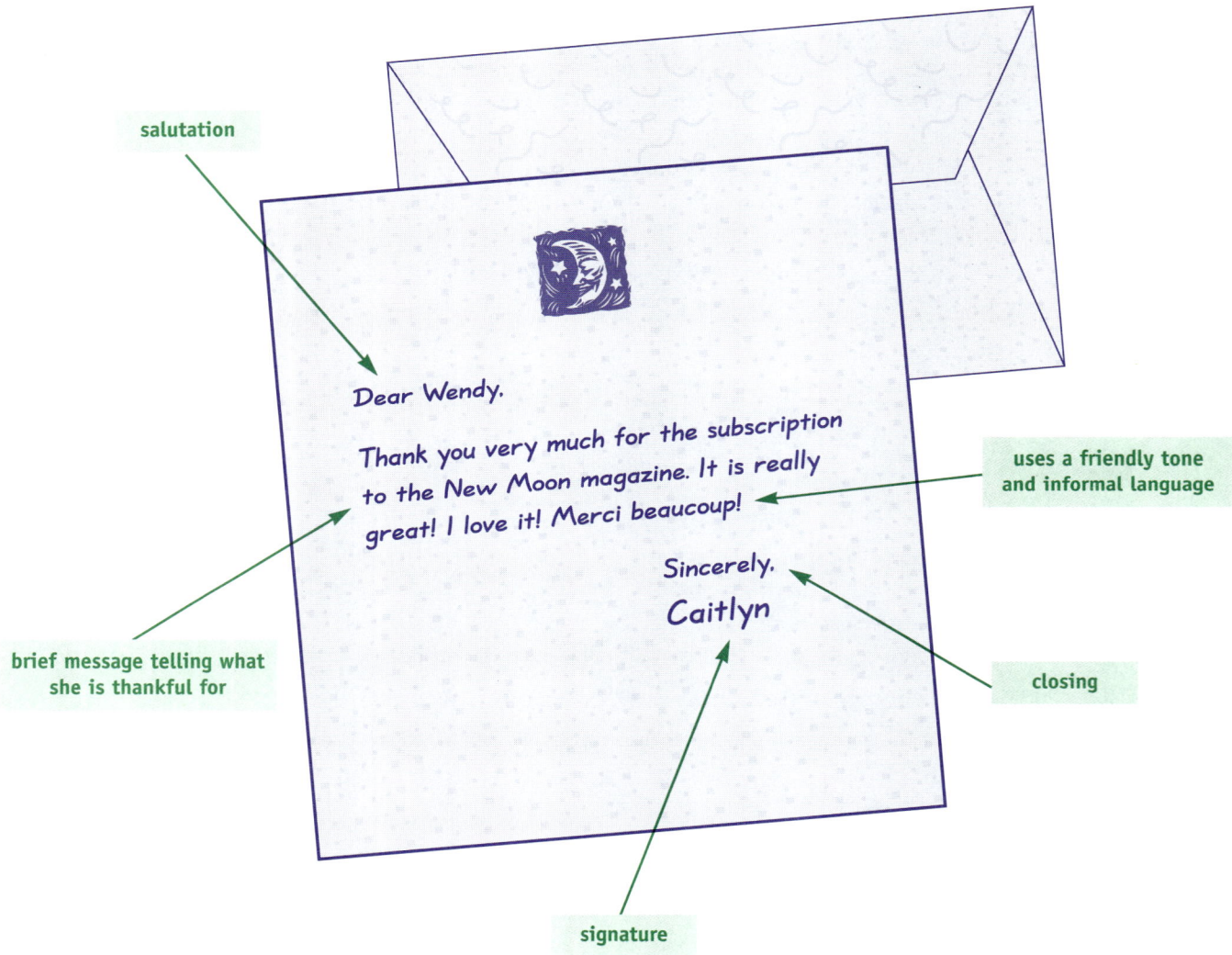

Features of Thank-You Notes

- Thank-you notes are brief and to the point.
- They are usually written in an informal style using a friendly tone.
- Thank-you notes are usually handwritten.
- They begin with a salutation such as "Dear" followed by the person's name.
- The date is usually included on a thank-you note.
- The body or message of the note is usually one or two paragraphs long and states what you are thanking the person for.
- The closing often says something nice such as "Love" or "Yours truly."
- Thank-you notes are signed.

Check These Out!

Reading thank-you notes can give you ideas for writing and creating your own. Examine thank-you notes you or your family have received and take a look at thank-you cards in card shops.

Choose an Idea

- Write a thank-you note to a friend or family member who has done something nice.
- Offer to write a thank-you note to a speaker who has visited your class or to the parent volunteers who work at your school.
- Send your thanks to a local hero who has done something special.
- Write a note to thank a friend and his or her family for having you over for dinner or for a sleepover.
- Create a thank-you note for a coach, an instructor, or a teacher who has helped you. Let special people know how much they are appreciated.
- Write a thank-you note to a classmate you worked with in a group.

Writing a Thank-You Note

Planning

1. Think about your audience. How would you normally talk to that person? You might be more casual with a family member than with a guest speaker.
2. What do you want to say? Think about what you would like to thank this person for and jot down some ideas. Consider the action or gift, and how it made you feel or how it helped you.

Skill Focus

Using **contractions** and **abbreviations** are two ways to save space in informal writing.

For lists of common abbreviations and contractions, see pages 181–182 and 184 of the Tool Kit.

Abbreviations may also be used when addressing the envelope of your note. Canada Post encourages people to use capital letters and no punctuation (including no periods with abbreviations) in addresses on mail. This helps them to process the mail more easily. For example:

SIMONE TAYLOR
2 PARK AVE EAST
BRANTFORD ON
N3T 2Z4

---

3 Study the way thank-you cards are written and designed. Take a look at the ones your family has received or check out some thank-you cards in a card shop.

4 Use a store-bought blank card or create your own special note. Be creative and design the card using coloured markers, stickers, and special lettering such as calligraphy. Add borders, illustrations, or cartoons.

Drafting

FOR MORE ABOUT THE WORD IN BOLD, SEE THE STYLE FILE.

1 Write a rough draft of your message on a separate piece of paper. Revise and edit it before you write the final copy on your card.

2 Write the message in a friendly **tone.** A thank-you note often sounds like something you would say in person or over the telephone.

3 Thank-you notes are usually quite brief, so choose your words carefully. Use abbreviations and contractions to save space. (See the Skill Focus.)

4 Be specific in your message. Choose accurate and interesting words to explain what in particular you liked, why you liked it, and, if it's a gift, how you plan on using it.

5 If you're sending your thank-you card through the mail, you'll need to address the envelope, include the postal code, and use a stamp.

Revising

Take another look at the draft of your thank-you note and consider the following.

- Does your message make sense? Is it brief and specific?
- Did you include everything you wanted to say?
- Have you written about the gift or about the reason you are sending the note?
- Have you mentioned why the gift is special or why you appreciated the favour so much?
- Have you written in a friendly, conversational tone?
- Did you use accurate and interesting words?
- Did you remember to date and sign the note?
- Are the mailing and return addresses correct?

Editing

FOR MORE ABOUT THE WORDS IN BOLD, SEE THE TOOL KIT.

Check your writing for

- correct **spelling**
- correct **abbreviations** and **contractions**
- complete **sentences**
- proper **punctuation** and **capitalization**

Publishing

- Write your revised and edited message on a blank card.
- Mail your thank-you note, or e-mail your message through the Internet.
- If you have written a thank-you note to the parent volunteers who work at your school, you could publish the note in the school newsletter.
- Send your thank-you note to a local hero to the editor of your local newspaper for publication.
- Turn your thank-you note to a friend or family member into a puzzle. Draw a puzzle design on the back of the page, cut it out, and put the pieces of the puzzle in the envelope.

Reflecting

- What did you learn about writing thank-you notes?
- Would you do anything differently the next time you write a thank-you note?
- What's the nicest thing anyone has ever done for you? How did you thank them?
- How does receiving a sincere thank-you make you feel?

COMPUTER LINK

Design your thank-you note on the computer. Choose an interesting typeface and add computer graphics to "jazz up" your note.

Friendly Letters

Want to get to know someone who lives in another country? Missing a friend or relative who's moved away? You can introduce yourself or keep in touch by writing a friendly letter. Friendly letters are a little like talking with someone, the conversation just takes longer. You can share some exciting news or tell about what's interesting or new in your life. Unlike a telephone call, a letter can be read over and over again and enjoyed for many years. And the best part is, when you write a letter, you often get one back!

Writing Goals

As you develop your friendly letter, ensure that you

- identify and model the textual and visual features of friendly letters
- relate events using narrative paragraphs
- include a variety of sentence types including questions, statements, and exclamatory sentences
- include correct punctuation—commas following the salutation and closing, and periods in abbreviations

Set one or two additional writing goals (skills you want to work on) for yourself.

Here is a letter Marina wrote to her friend Jaime.

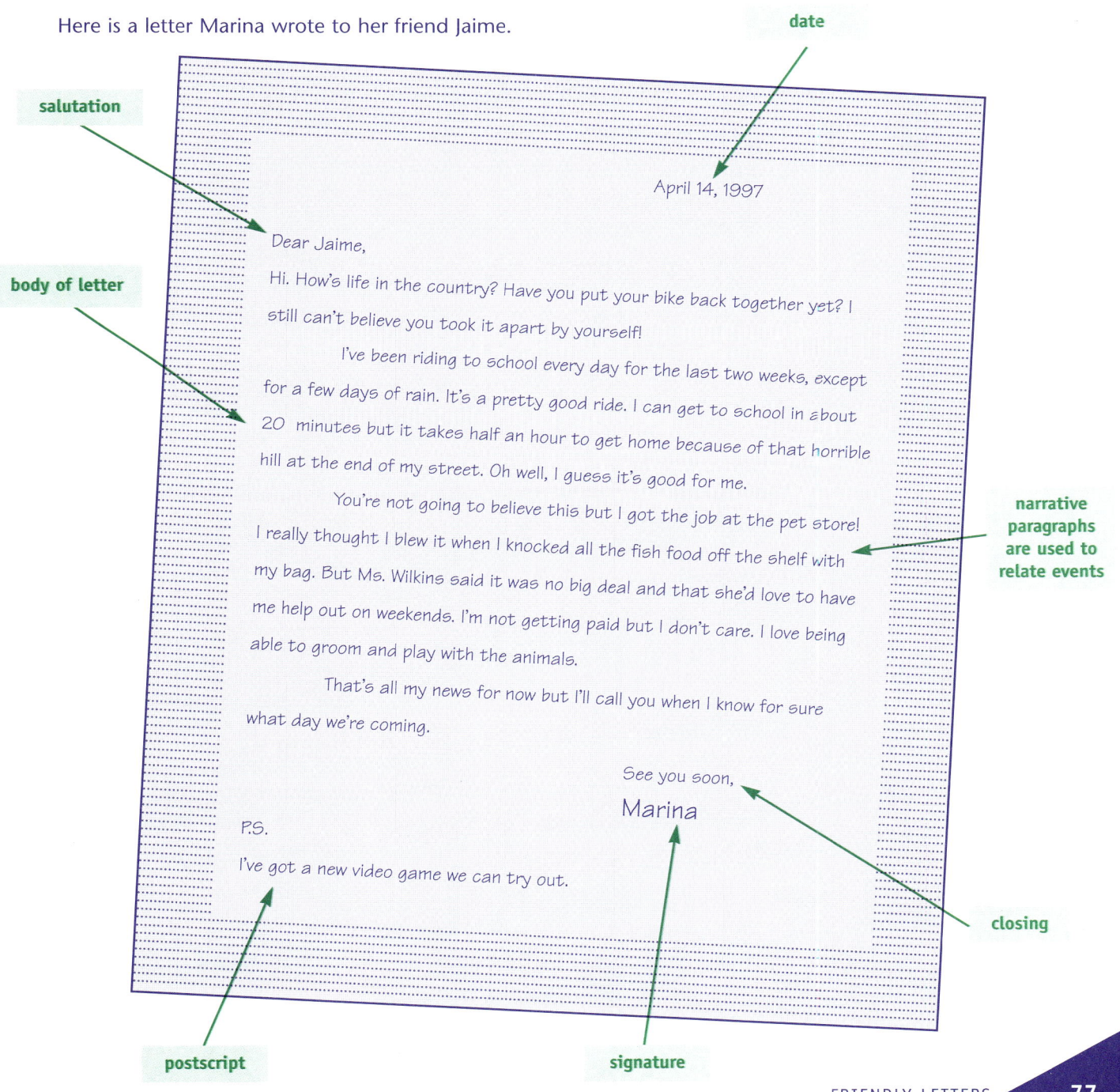

salutation · **date** · **body of letter** · **narrative paragraphs are used to relate events** · **postscript** · **signature** · **closing**

FRIENDLY LETTERS

Check These Out!

Looking at how authors write letters in books can help you write your own.
- *Letters from a Lady Rancher* by Monica Hopkins
- *Dear Bruce Springsteen* by Kevin Major
- *The Mennyms* by Sylvia Waugh
- *Letters in the Wilderness* by Aranka Siegal

INFO

If you would like help finding a pen pal, write to one of these organizations in Canada.

THE PEN PAL POST
559 PAPE AVE
TORONTO ON
M4K 3R5

CORRESPONDENCE CANADA
2695 MCWILLIS AVE
MONTREAL PQ
H4R 1M5

Features of Friendly Letters

- Friendly letters have five main parts.
  - The heading usually includes your address and the date. The address may be left out if your reader knows you well.
  - The salutation usually begins with "Dear" followed by the person's name and a comma.
  - The body of the letter includes your thoughts, feelings, and ideas written in short paragraphs.
  - The closing of the letter usually says something nice, such as "Take care," "See you soon," or "All my love," and is followed by a comma.
  - The letter ends with your signature.
- Abbreviations are often used in the heading address.
- The body is usually written in a conversational tone using friendly language and an informal style.
- Friendly letters may include a P.S. (postscript) or "after writing." Often people remember something they want to say after they have closed the letter.
- Additional items such as photographs, sketches, cartoons, articles, and quotations are sometimes included in a friendly letter.

Choose an Idea

- Become a pen pal. Many people find that being a pen pal leads to lifelong friendships.
- Write a letter to a friend who has moved away or to a relative who lives out of town. Be sure to highlight all of your activities and news.
- Write a letter that is ongoing. Write a little bit every day and then send it after a week of entries.
- Write a friendly letter that might have been written by an historical figure. What event or significant time in history will you choose? Try using the language of that time and place.
- Write a letter between two fictional characters. What would Romeo write to Juliet, or Superman to Lois Lane?
- Write a friendly letter to a person from history or literature.

Writing a Friendly Letter

Planning

1. Decide whom you want to write to.
2. Jot down all of the ideas you want to include in your letter. You might share a funny story, describe something you like to do, or tell what's been happening in your life. If you keep a diary, you could use it to help you remember things.
3. Reread the last letter you received and think of a few questions for your friend to answer.

Drafting

FOR MORE ABOUT THE WORD IN BOLD, SEE THE STYLE FILE.

1. Start with one of the ideas on your list. You might write about the most recent events first, or begin with the funniest story, or answer some of the questions the other person asked in a recent letter.
2. Consider your audience. How would you talk to that person if you were face to face? Your **tone** might be more conversational with a friend than with a new pen pal or your grandparents.
3. Make your letter interesting, funny, and lively. Use descriptive language such as colourful adjectives and adverbs to make your experiences come alive for your reader.
4. Keep your letter easy to read by beginning a new paragraph each time you start a new idea. Use narrative paragraphs to relate events or tell stories. (For more about narrative paragraphs, see the Skill Focus.)
5. Include drawings, photographs, or articles to make your letter into an "event" that your audience will love to receive and read.
6. Use a variety of sentence styles. Ask questions, make statements, and include exclamatory sentences to spice up your letter.
7. Number your pages if you use more than one page.

Skill Focus

A paragraph is a group of sentences that express a single idea. **Narrative paragraphs** are a special type of paragraph used to relate events or to tell a story. Narrative paragraphs are written using a consistent point of view; they include an opening sentence that sets the scene for the story or event; and they usually provide details in the order they occurred.

For more about narrative paragraphs, see page 173 of the Tool Kit.

COMPUTER LINK

People who send e-mail (electronic mail) through their computers call regular mail "snail mail." While a regular letter might take over a week to reach its destination across the world, an e-mail letter travels this distance in minutes through your telephone lines.

For more about writing an e-mail message, see page 158 of the Tool Kit.

8 Choose a closing that says something nice such as "Yours truly" or "Sincerely" to a friend or pen pal, and "Love" to a family member.

9 Write the person's address on the front of the envelope and your return address in the upper left corner or on the back. (Canada Post asks that you use capital letters and no punctuation in addresses on letters and postcards. This helps them to process the mail more easily.)

Revising

Before you mail your letter, ask yourself these questions.

- Have you included all of the parts of a friendly letter—heading, salutation, body, closing, and signature?
- Does your letter make sense? Did you include everything you wanted to say? Did you ask some questions for the person to respond to in his or her next letter?
- Have you used a friendly, conversational tone, as if you were talking to the person you're writing to?
- Have you used narrative paragraphs to tell stories and relate events?
- Is your letter filled with interesting details and lively language that will appeal to your reader?
- If you forgot to tell something important, did you add a P.S. (postscript) or use the P.S. to ask for a return letter or to stress something important?

Editing

FOR MORE ABOUT THE WORDS IN BOLD, SEE THE TOOL KIT.

Check your writing for

- descriptive **adjectives** and **adverbs**
- proper **paragraph** structure
- proper **punctuation** and **capitalization**
- correct **spelling**
- correct mailing and return addresses

Publishing

- Mail, fax, or e-mail a good copy of your letter. Everyone loves to get mail.
- Send your letter introducing yourself to a new pen pal.
- Include your historical letter in a history project.
- Create a bulletin-board display to share your fictional letters, or put them together in a book.
- Cut out interesting articles, good jokes, or funny stories from magazines and newspapers, and send them along with your letter.
- Record your letter on a cassette and send it. Include a recent photograph of yourself.

Reflecting

- What types of things can you learn about people through their letter-writing?
- Why do you think writing good letters is considered by some people to be an "art"?
- Think of two or three things you can do next time to make your letters more exciting.

INFO

You can personalize a letter by making your own stationery. Think about the type of letter you are writing, the historical time period, or who the fictional author of the letter is. Then let your imagination run free with illustration and calligraphy ideas!

FRIENDLY LETTERS

Advertising

- **Print Advertisements**
- **Jingles**

We're bombarded by advertising. Advertisements appear in magazines and newspapers, they're on TV and radio, they're on the World Wide Web, and even at the movie theatre. They're on videotapes, billboards, flyers, and promotions. They're everywhere!

If advertisements are so common, why do so many still catch our attention? Why can't we just tune them all out? We can't because they are designed and written specifically to grab and hold our attention. Some are so catchy that we find ourselves singing along!

To create a good advertisement, you must know your product, know your audience, and know how to reach that audience in order to convince them to "buy into" your product, service, or idea. A good advertisement, whether we read it, watch it, or listen to it, is difficult to ignore.

Print Advertisements

Advertisements can be seen and heard everywhere—on TV and radio, on signs and billboards, in magazines and newspapers, in flyers and junk mail, on the Internet, and even on the clothes we wear and bags we carry. Advertisements try to persuade us to buy a product or service, believe in an idea, or change our behaviour.

Print advertisements attract our attention with clever designs, striking images, and effective slogans. Everything in an advertisement has been put there for a purpose. Advertisements are very carefully crafted and there are no mistakes in them. Some print advertisements provide information in a straightforward way. Other advertisements use art, pictures, or photographs to create an image that appeals to our senses and emotions. Some advertisements use famous people or cartoon characters to sell a product. In any form, advertisements are a powerful, persuasive tool.

Writing Goals

As you develop your print advertisement, ensure that you
- identify and model the features of print advertisements
- write an effective slogan to appeal to your target audience
- experiment with sentence styles to establish a specific tone
- experiment with lettering, graphics, colour, and layout

Set one or two additional writing goals (skills you want to work on) for yourself.

Examine this print advertisement of the future that Joshua wrote.

Features of Print Advertisements

- Print advertisements send messages to convince the consumer to buy a product, an idea, or a service.
- Print advertisements use carefully selected words and images that appeal to people's emotions or reason.
- They are designed to appeal to a specific target audience.
- Print advertisements often promise to make life better in some way if the consumer buys the product or service.
- Slogans (short, catchy phrases) are sometimes used.
- Gimmicky spelling or symbols are often used to attract attention to the advertisement.
- A variety of print sizes and styles, and colours are used to make important information "pop out."
- Visual features may be arranged by combining two contrasting images to create a centre of interest; for example, "before" and "after" photographs. This is called juxtaposition.

Choose an Idea

- Design a print advertisement to promote a sports product that would appeal to the students in your school; for example, in-line skates, a skateboard, a bike, or a basketball.
- Think of an issue that is important to you, such as doing volunteer work, and write an advertisement to promote your message. You might create two advertisements—one directed at classmates and the other at adults.
- Create a print advertisement for a product of the future. What products or services might be advertised 100 years from now?
- Design an advertisement to advertise a school dance or another event at your school or in your community.
- With a group of friends, develop a print advertising campaign. You could advertise something real such as a product you believe in, or you could research a famous politician or hero and create an imaginary campaign to promote his or her leadership.

Check These Out!

Look for interesting print advertisements around your school and your neighbourhood—on billboards, flyers, and posters—and on the Internet, and in magazines and newspapers.

Skill Focus

Juxtaposition is the impact created by placing two contrasting ideas or images side by side. For example, a photograph of a face with pimples beside the same face without a blemish.

The same effect can be achieved with words and ideas; for example, "the stressed-out worker" and "the relaxed vacationer."

For more about juxtaposition, see page 142 of the Style File.

Writing a Print Advertisement

Planning

1 Decide what you want to advertise. Is there something you feel strongly about? Will you advertise a product, an idea, or a service?
2 Determine who your target audience is. This is the group of people your advertisement is aimed at. Jot down some notes about your target audience and refer to these notes as you write your advertisement. What kinds of words and images will catch their attention?

Drafting

FOR MORE ABOUT THE WORDS IN BOLD, SEE THE STYLE FILE.

1 Write the main idea of what you want to present in your advertisement and list four or five reasons or facts to support it.
   - Include some words and phrases to describe your product—its features and what makes it a good product to buy.
   - What quality or feature of your product or service will "hook" your audience? Will it be the price, image, or something else?
   - Think about what claims or promises you want to make.
2 Develop a **slogan** for the product or service. A slogan is a short, catchy phrase such as Nike's "Just Do It," which suggests that you can do anything when sporting a pair of Nike running shoes.
3 Decide on the **tone** of your advertisement. Will it be straightforward and business-like, funny or dramatic? Use a variety of sentence styles in your copy to give your advertisement the right tone. (See the Skill Focus for more about sentence styles.)
4 Decide if you'll use photographs or graphics in the advertisement. If you're advertising a product, you'll want to show a photograph or an illustration of the product.
5 Plan the layout of your advertisement. Think about ways to make it appealing to your target audience. Experiment with the layout before putting in a lot of details.

Skill Focus

Different **sentence styles** can be used to convey different tones. For example, short, simple sentences can be exciting and rhythmic and may be used to "punch up" your copy (the text). Complex, descriptive sentences can seem more trustworthy and serious.

For more about sentence styles, see page 167 of the Tool Kit.

- What size will you make the advertisement?
- What colours and lettering will you use?
- If you're advertising a product, where will you place an image of the product?
- Where will you put your slogan?
- How will you arrange the words and the art together?
- How much white space will you leave? Some empty space is important to balance out the amount of text and images in the advertisement.

Revising

Once you have decided on your layout, ask yourself these questions.

- Will the advertisement appeal to your target audience?
- Is the message clear? Is it convincing?
- Do you have too little, too much, or just enough information?
- Does the tone work with the message of your advertisement?
- Is the advertisement balanced with a good amount of white space, text, and visual information?
- Does the most important information "pop out"?
- Have you used lettering, graphics, and colour effectively?
- Have you tested your advertisement on friends or someone from your target audience to get his or her reactions and suggestions?

Editing

FOR MORE ABOUT THE WORDS IN BOLD, SEE THE TOOL KIT.

Check your writing for

- correct **spelling** (Make sure that words in "gimmicky" spelling are easily recognizable to the reader.)
- proper **punctuation**

INFO

A **layout** is a rough sketch used to help you plan your advertisement. It doesn't have a lot of detail, but shows where the words and art will go. Designing a layout lets you try different arrangements of text, pictures, and white space before you make your final decision. Experimenting with different layouts can help you find the most exciting and interesting design possible.

COMPUTER LINK

Design your print advertisement on a computer. Experiment with various sizes and styles of type. Choose art from clip art files, if they are available, or create your own images using a drawing program.

INFO !!!

Writing advertising copy for TV, radio, the Internet, magazines, newspapers, and billboards is a competitive and highly creative job. If you discover that you have a talent for writing advertisements, and enjoy it, a career in advertising might be something to consider.

Publishing

- Display your advertising campaign on a bulletin board in your classroom.
- Display the advertisements and vote on the most persuasive or the most visually appealing.
- Display your advertisement for a school event in the hallway, resource centre, library, or cafeteria.
- If you created an advertisement on a particular issue, send it to a related organization that may be able to use it in their campaign.

Reflecting

- What new techniques did you learn from creating a print advertisement?
- What is your favourite professional print advertisement? What makes this advertisement work for you?
- Why do you think print advertisements are an effective way to persuade people to "buy into" a product or service?

Jingles

Jingles are musical advertisements that use about 30 seconds of radio or television time to promote a product, a service, or an idea to a target audience. Though simple, jingles are highly technical and persuasive tools of advertising. They attract the listeners' attention and appeal to their emotions and senses by creating a specific image or feeling.

Jingles are a popular form of advertising because the short, catchy phrases and simple music make them easy to remember. A jingle is usually the first clue to help the listener recognize an ad and its product.

Writing jingles can be a lot of fun. By combining your skills of persuasion with an unexpected approach and a catchy tune, you can create a jingle that others find impossible to ignore or to stop singing!

Writing Goals

As you develop your jingle, ensure that you
- identify and model the features of jingles
- deliver an entertaining message in clear, concise language
- experiment with techniques such as repetition and onomatopoeia
- combine music with words

Set one or two additional writing goals (skills you want to work on) for yourself.

Diane wrote this jingle to appeal to children. Brady wrote his jingle as a public service announcement for teenagers. Do you recognize the tunes?

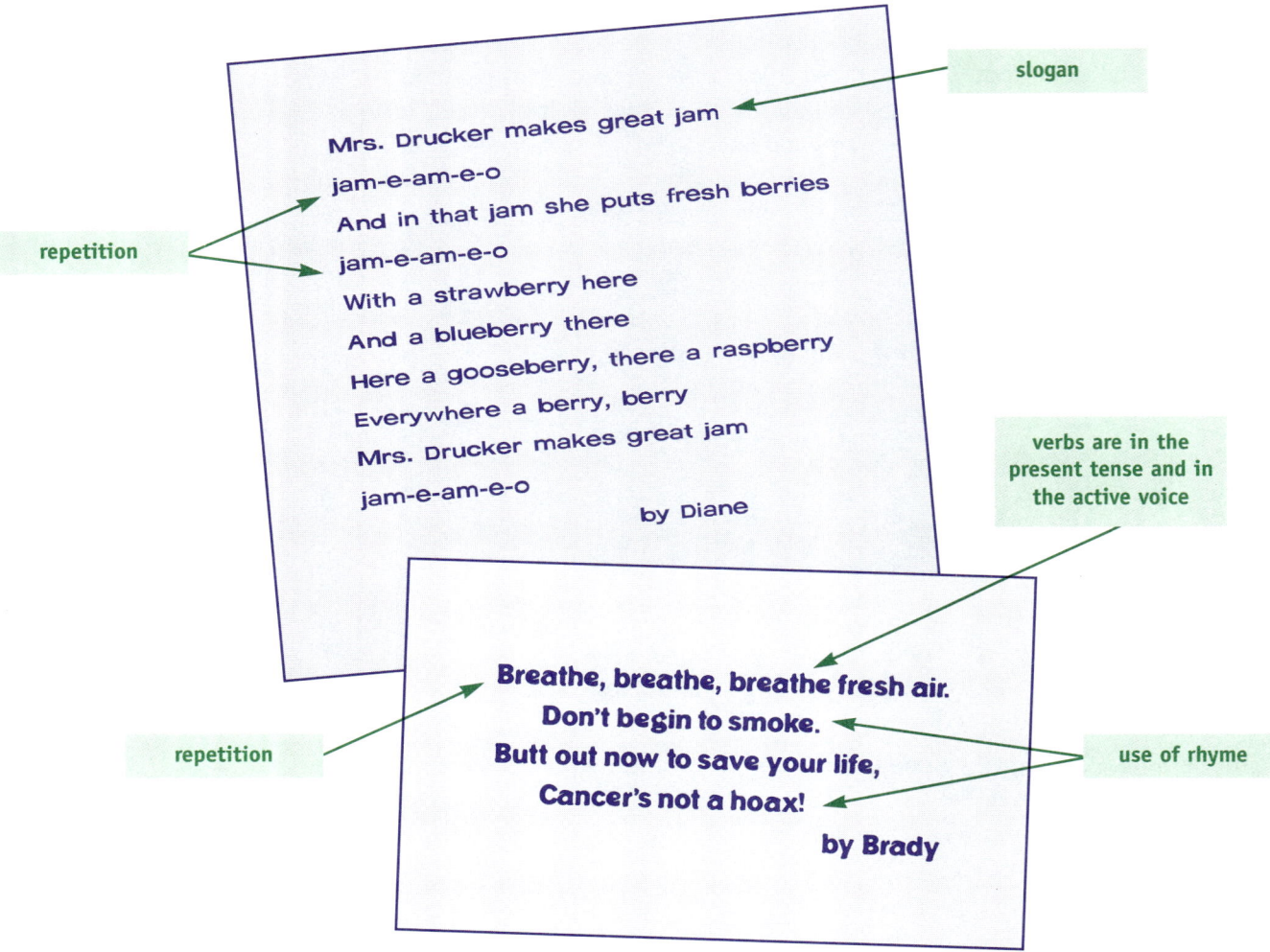

Features of Jingles

- Jingles are advertisements set to music.
- They send a message that tries to sell a product, a service, or an idea.
- The message is simple but powerful and usually has a "feel good" tone.
- The message is very clear and brief, but every word is important.
- Jingles have catchy phrases called slogans that sum up the message of the jingle in one line.
- Simple, original tunes, familiar music, and/or other types of sound effects add to the appeal of the jingle.

Check These Out!

Listen to jingles on radio and television advertisements. Which ones do you think work best? Why?

Choose an Idea

- Choose one of your favourite products, such as shampoo or a soft drink, and create a jingle that would appeal to a teenage audience.
- If you or a friend are running for a position, for example, for president of the drama club, create a jingle for your campaign.
- Think about the image of your favourite sports team and create a jingle that captures it.
- Create a jingle for your home answering machine and use sound effects or music to add to the appeal.
- Create a jingle to advertise a school team or event.

Writing a Jingle

Planning

1. Decide on the subject of your jingle.
2. Think about the kind of image and feelings you want to create to "sell" your product or service and jot down your ideas. Try approaching your subject from an unexpected angle. Be as wacky as you want to be—being different will get your jingle noticed.

Skill Focus

Jingles often use **rhymes** such as rhyming couplets in their slogans. These couplets have rhyming words at the end of each line, and express a complete thought.
For example:
 A Mars Bar a day
 At work, rest, or play!

Jingles also create memorable messages by creating **rhythm** in a sequence of words.
For example:
 Always so good for so little! Swiss Chalet

For more about rhyme and rhythm, see pages 148 and 149 of the Style File and Couplets and Quatrains on pages 95–100.

Drafting

FOR MORE ABOUT THE WORDS IN BOLD, SEE THE STYLE FILE.

1 Think about a short, catchy phrase or **slogan** that sums up the image or message of your product. For example, with the slogan "You deserve a break today," McDonald's suggests that buying their food makes life easier for you. (See the Skill Focus for more about using rhymes and rhythm in slogans.)

2 Once you have a slogan, think about the rest of your jingle. It should build up logically and clearly to the main message of your slogan. For ideas, look at your jot notes to determine the image or feelings you want to create with your jingle.

3 Consider using **onomatopoeia** (words that imitate sounds) to bring specific images to the listener. Examples of onomatopoeia include "clatter," "hum," "gurgle," and "ripple."

4 Repetition is another useful tool in jingles. You can repeat words or images to strengthen the message, and repeat sounds using **alliteration** to add flow to your jingle. (See the Skill Focus on alliteration on page 93.)

5 Now set your words to music. Some jingles use popular tunes that the audience is already familiar with. If you decide to use a popular tune, choose a simple one that you can play or copy. Or you could create your own tune.

Revising

- Does your jingle make sense? Is it a complete thought?
- Are your words effective and is the message brief and clear?
- Are there any words you need to change, add, or take out to improve your jingle?
- Are you satisfied with the sense of rhythm and the rhyme scheme, if you have chosen to use one?
- Have you listened to your jingle on a tape recorder to hear its effect?
- Does the music or tune work with the words to create the desired effect?
- Ask classmates or an adult to say the jingle. Can they say it easily, in the way you want it to sound? What suggestions do they have for making your jingle more effective?

Editing

FOR MORE ABOUT THE WORDS IN BOLD, SEE THE TOOL KIT.

Check your writing for

- **verbs** in the **present tense** and in the **active voice**
- proper **spelling** so that words are pronounced correctly (Use a dictionary to check the pronunciation of unfamiliar words.)

Publishing

- If you wrote a jingle for yourself or a friend who is running for a position, you could put it to music, record it, and play it during the campaign.
- Advertise a school team or event by asking permission to put your jingle on the morning announcements.
- Record your jingle on your home answering machine and see what kind of a response you get from callers.
- Play or perform your jingle for classmates.

Reflecting

- What new techniques did you learn as you created your jingle?
- What were the responses of the people who listened to it?
- What would you do differently if you wrote another jingle?
- Why do you think jingles are effective selling/advertising tools?

Skill Focus

The repetition of sounds, especially of consonants at the beginning of words, is called **alliteration**. Any repetition of sound, either within a word such as "bumblebee" or within a phrase or sentence, adds emphasis to the words and strengthens the impact of the message.

For more about alliteration, see page 134 of the Style File.

Poetry

- *Couplets and Quatrains*
- *Found Poetry*

Poetry offers a different way to explore and represent ideas, feelings, images, and stories. Poetry can take many forms. Poems can be written in a set number of lines and syllables, such as haiku or a cinquain, or written in rhyme, such as quatrains and limericks. Poems are also written in free verse form where writers use line arrangements to create a natural rhythm to the poem. Or poems may have special shapes and patterns, such as list poems and acrostics.

Each type of poetry has its own form and style, but all poems are a wonderful means of entertaining your audience while reflecting on and interpreting the world you see around you, as well as the world within.

Explore the world of poetry and you'll soon find a form that inspires you.

Couplets and Quatrains

Rhyme easily finds its way into language. You hear rhyme in lyrics (the written words of songs), in advertisements, and in musical jingles. You read rhymes in greeting cards you get for birthdays and other occasions.

There are many forms of rhyming poems. In this section you can explore rhyming couplets and quatrains. Rhymed poems offer an opportunity to experiment with the sounds of words and with the beats or rhythms created by the combination of those words.

Each type of rhyme offers you a special way to reflect—to be funny, musical, or thoughtful. It can give you a chance to share experiences, to express feelings, or to create images that offer a window on a moment of action, beauty, or fun. Writing couplets and quatrains gives you the chance to give words life.

Writing Goals

As you develop your couplets and quatrains, ensure that you

- identify and model the features of couplets and quatrains
- use webs to develop ideas for poems
- experiment with rhyme and rhythm
- use active verbs and specific nouns

Set one or two additional writing goals (skills you want to work on) for yourself.

Read these poems written by Nicholas and Jennifer.

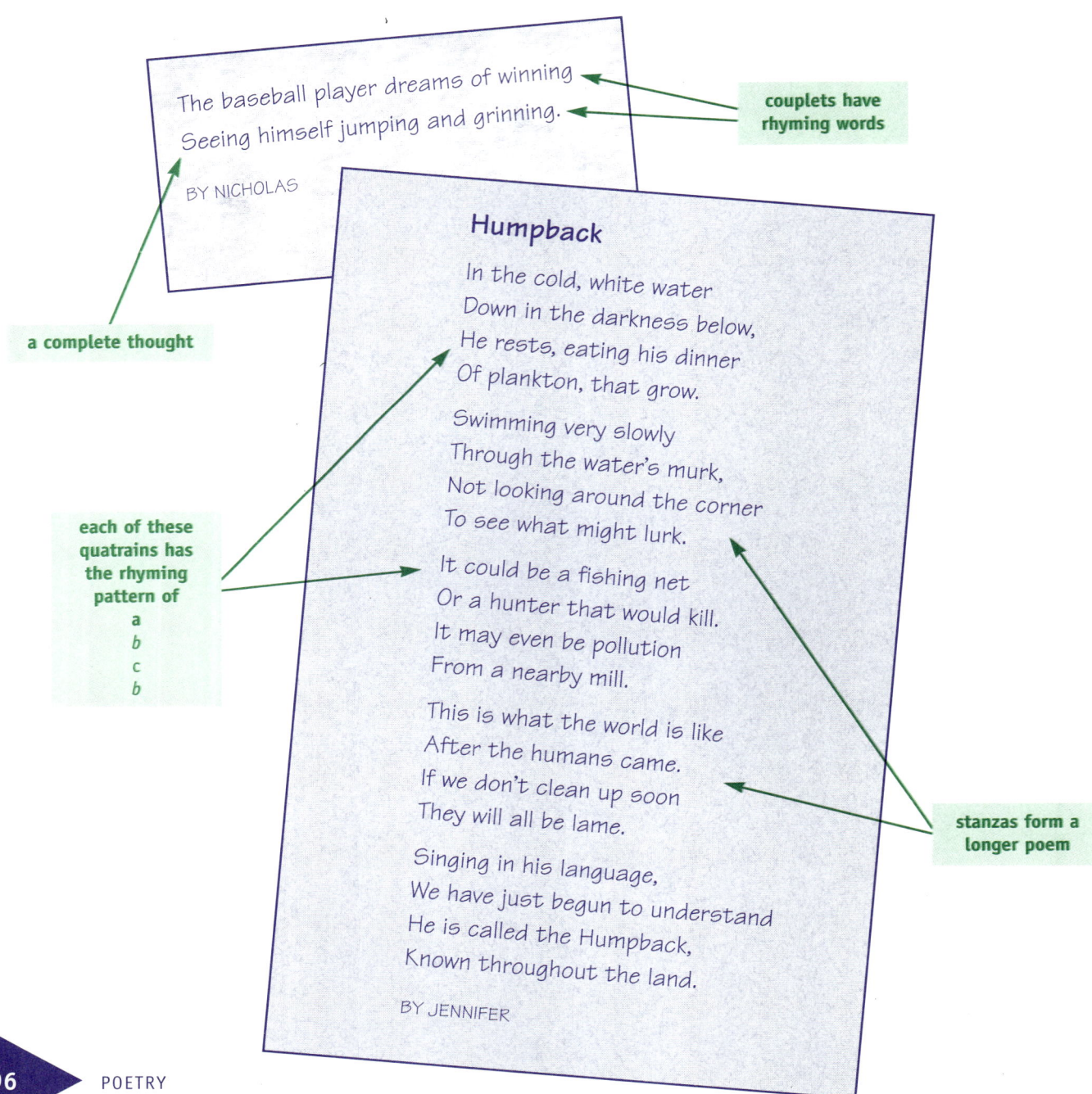

The baseball player dreams of winning
Seeing himself jumping and grinning.

BY NICHOLAS

couplets have rhyming words

a complete thought

Humpback

In the cold, white water
Down in the darkness below,
He rests, eating his dinner
Of plankton, that grow.

Swimming very slowly
Through the water's murk,
Not looking around the corner
To see what might lurk.

It could be a fishing net
Or a hunter that would kill.
It may even be pollution
From a nearby mill.

This is what the world is like
After the humans came.
If we don't clean up soon
They will all be lame.

Singing in his language,
We have just begun to understand
He is called the Humpback,
Known throughout the land.

BY JENNIFER

each of these quatrains has the rhyming pattern of
a
b
c
b

stanzas form a longer poem

Features of Couplets and Quatrains

- The first word of the poem along with the first word of each line is generally capitalized.
- Punctuation may or may not be included.

Couplets

- have two lines
- have rhyming words at the end of each line
- are a complete thought

    *The little birds sit in their nest and **beg**,*
    *All mouth that once had been all **egg**.* —Anonymous

- have a rhythm pattern determined by the number of beats in a line.

Quatrains

- have four lines
- are a complete thought
- have rhyming words at the ends of the lines to make the rhyming pattern
- have rhyming patterns that can vary

    | LINE 1 | *The rain is raining all **around**,* | a |
    | LINE 2 | *It falls on field and **tree**,* | b |
    | LINE 3 | *It rains on the umbrellas here,* | c |
    | LINE 4 | *And on the ships at **sea**.* | b |

    —Robert Louis Stevenson

    To show the rhyming pattern we use letters—a's rhyme with a's and b's rhyme with b's. Here are some other patterns.

LINE 1	a	a	a	a
LINE 2	a	b	b	b
LINE 3	b	a	b	c
LINE 4	b	b	a	a

- have a rhythm pattern determined by the number of beats in a line

Check These Out!

Read some poetry by professional poets to get ideas for your own poetry.

- *The Poems of Jeremy Bloom* by Gordon Korman and Bernice Korman
- *Doggerel* by Sheila Daton
- *Save the World for Me* by Maxine Tynes
- *Side by Side* and *Poetry Express* selected by James Barry

Skill Focus

A common **rhythm** pattern in a line is three to five stressed syllables or beats (strongly pronounced) combined with unstressed syllables (pronounced weakly).

A regular rhythm is repeated in each line or alternated in a pattern throughout the poem.

For more about rhythm, see page 149 of the Style File.

INFO

Quatrains or couplets are called "stanzas" when they are linked together to make a longer poem. Stanzas are groups of lines in a poem that have a repeating rhythm and rhyme pattern, and the same number of lines.

Choose an Idea

- Write a poem about a change you've experienced in your relationships with others, or about other changes you've witnessed while growing up.
- From personal or family photographs, or from a magazine, select a shot that shows strong feeling. Take the point of view of one of the people in the photograph and write a couplet or a quatrain to express that person's feelings.
- Write a poem about an issue or subject that is important to you, such as being given responsibility, being an older or younger sibling, peer pressure, violence on TV, or any topic that sparks your interest.
- Write some humorous couplets or quatrains.
- Write a couplet or quatrain based on something you like to do. Think of your favourite hobby or the sport you like the best.
- With a partner, choose an issue of world importance, such as endangered habitats, gender issues, hunger, or global warming, and write a couplet or quatrain to state your concerns. Try writing a series of poems on this theme.

Writing a Couplet or Quatrain

Planning

1 Choose the type of poem you want to write—couplet or quatrain.
2 Decide on a topic for your poem. To get ideas, brainstorm a list of interesting subjects and jot them down.

Summer

dripping ice-cream cone — blown, drone, grown, known, lone, phone, throne, zone

warm rain — brain, chain, drain, gain, lane, pane, plane

hot nights — bites, fights, flights, kites, lights, sights

3 Choose the topic that gives you the most ideas, and web or list the images and words that come to mind. What details can you think of? What memories, actions, or emotions come to mind? Think of sounds, smells, tastes, and how the topic makes you feel.

4 Select the words and phrases you like the best and list some rhyming words for them.

Drafting

FOR MORE ABOUT THE WORDS IN BOLD, SEE THE STYLE FILE.

1 Check the features for your couplet or quatrain. Note the **rhyme** scheme. How many rhyming lines do you need?

2 Develop the **rhythm** pattern for the lines of your poem. Choose a regular number of beats for each line, or a pattern of beats for alternating lines.

3 Indicate action using precise verbs. Use the present tense of verbs to make your poetry feel more immediate and real to your audience.

4 Give clear descriptions using active verbs and specific nouns. (See the Skill Focus.)

5 Include a title to grab your reader's attention.

Revising

Read your poem aloud to yourself and consider these points as you revise.

- Does your poem match the features of a couplet or quatrain?
- Does your poem make sense? Is it a complete thought?
- Have you written in a natural style? Does your poem sound like you?
- Check the rhyming pattern. Do the rhyming lines work for your topic and express the feeling of your poem?
- Is the rhythm pattern consistent?
- Have you chosen the best active verbs and specific nouns for your poem?
- Have you replaced any overused or repeated words with alternatives? Use a thesaurus to find a variety of synonyms.

Skill Focus

Use active **verbs** and specific **nouns** to add meaning and detail to your writing. For example:

I glimpsed the pond through the trees

is much more clear and interesting than

I saw the water through the trees.

Using active verbs and specific nouns helps you avoid unnecessary adjectives and adverbs that can "clutter up" your writing.

For more about verbs and nouns, see pages 160–162 of the Tool Kit.

Editing

FOR MORE ABOUT THE WORDS IN BOLD, SEE THE TOOL KIT.

Check your writing for

- proper **punctuation,** if included
- correct and consistent use of **capitalization**
- a line space between each stanza
- correct **spelling**

Publishing

- Write your poem on an index card or record it on a cassette tape and share it with a partner or small group of students in your class.
- Use a poster format and illustrate your poem. Display completed pieces on a classroom or school bulletin board. Give your poster an eye-catching title.
- Make computer printouts of your poem and give copies to friends and family.
- E-mail your poem to a friend or pen pal.
- With a partner or small group, publish an anthology of rhyming poems on a similar theme.
- Submit your poem for publication in your school paper or to a writing contest.

Reflecting

- What do you like about writing rhyming poems?
- What can poetry tell you about the writer?
- What is it about poetry that makes it different from narrative?
- What suggestions would you offer others for writing a couplet or a quatrain?

Found Poetry

Have you ever wondered what makes a poem, a poem? Canadian writer John Robert Colombo, a lover of found poetry, suggests that poems can be found everywhere in the world of print. Sometimes you just don't recognize them!

A found poem begins as a collection of words, phrases, or sentences that are removed from their context—from a magazine article, an advertisement, a headline, or even a street sign. The text might be chosen because it is thought provoking, creates a vivid image, has poetic appeal, or simply because it catches your eye. The poem is "found" when you rework the line and word arrangement to reveal a new awareness, meaning, or emphasis for these lines of text.

Writing a found poem offers you the opportunity to rearrange and put together words to highlight a specific rhythm, mood, image, or feeling. So go ahead and find the poems that lie hidden at your fingertips.

Writing Goals

As you develop your found poem, ensure that you

- identify and model the features of found poems
- select appropriate text from a range of media
- experiment with the content, structure, and voice of the text
- use capitalization and punctuation to give meaning

Set one or two additional writing goals (skills you want to work on) for yourself.

Alexander and Robert wrote these found poems based on text from a *National Geographic* magazine.

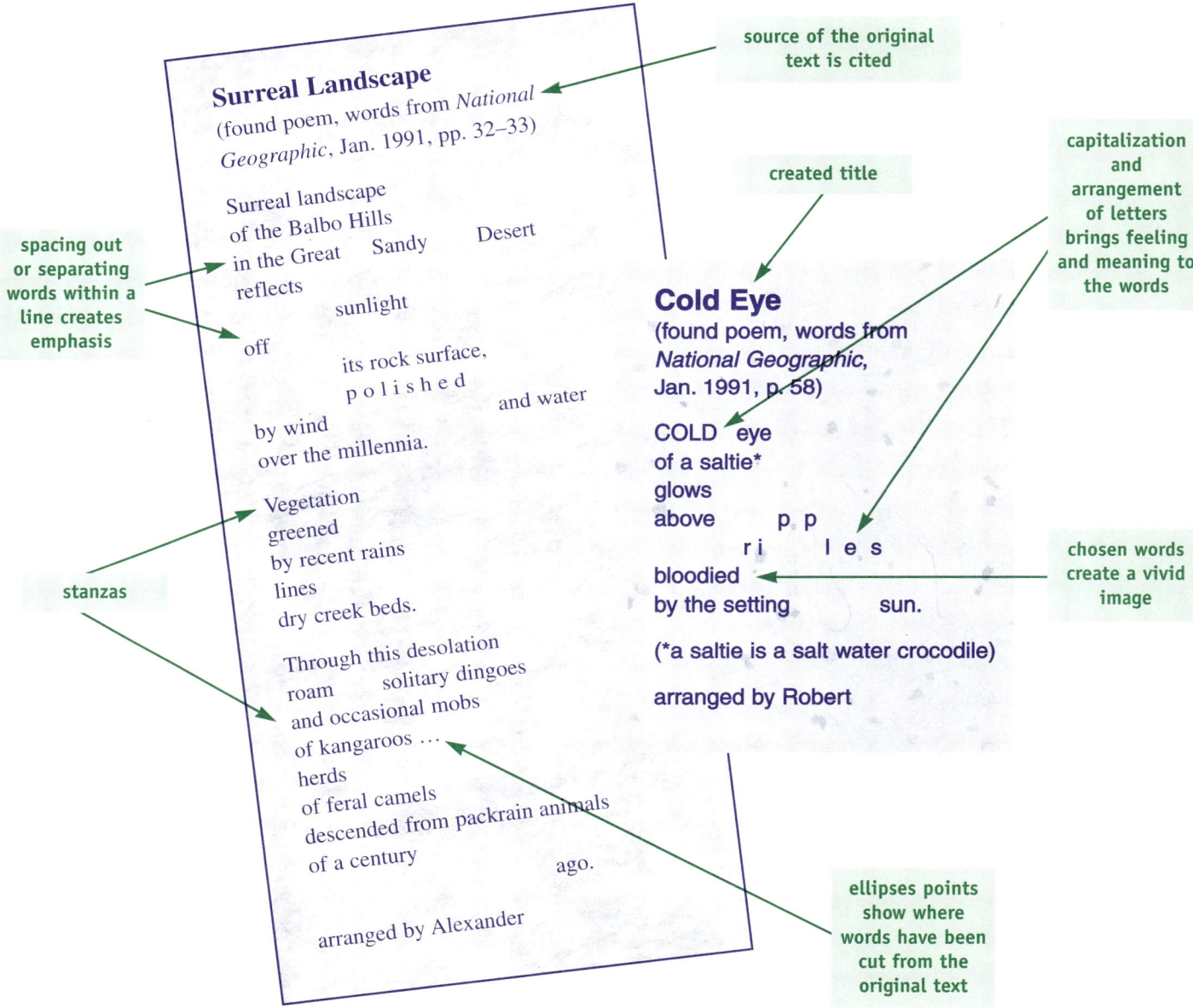

Surreal Landscape
(found poem, words from *National Geographic*, Jan. 1991, pp. 32–33)

Surreal landscape
of the Balbo Hills
in the Great   Sandy   Desert
reflects
            sunlight
    off
            its rock surface,
            p o l i s h e d
by wind   and water
over the millennia.

Vegetation
greened
by recent rains
lines
dry creek beds.

Through this desolation
roam   solitary dingoes
and occasional mobs
of kangaroos …
herds
of feral camels
descended from packrain animals
of a century   ago.

arranged by Alexander

Cold Eye
(found poem, words from *National Geographic*, Jan. 1991, p. 58)

COLD eye
of a saltie*
glows
above   p p
            r i   l e s
bloodied
by the setting   sun.

(*a saltie is a salt water crocodile)

arranged by Robert

- source of the original text is cited
- created title
- capitalization and arrangement of letters brings feeling and meaning to the words
- spacing out or separating words within a line creates emphasis
- chosen words create a vivid image
- stanzas
- ellipses points show where words have been cut from the original text

Features of Found Poetry

- The content can come from any written text, such as a story, an advertisement, or a caption from a magazine article—any words or phrases that catch your attention.
- Words and lines are arranged to bring out a special meaning, feeling, rhythm, or emphasis.
- Punctuation may be added, removed, or left as it appears in the original text.
- Capitalization of the first word in a line, or the first word of a stanza, is optional. However, capitalization should be consistent.
- The source of original text is cited if applicable. (For example, the name of the article, *The Globe and Mail,* July 23, 1993, p. A2.)

Check These Out!

Look for some of these poetry collections in your library to see how other writers arrange their found poetry.
- *Do Whales Jump at Night?* edited by Florence McNeil
- *The Mackenzie Poems; John Toronto; John Robert Colombo Selected Poems;* and *Made in Canada* by John Robert Colombo
- *Out Loud* by Eve Merriam

Choose an Idea

Create a found poem using text found in the world around you.

- Choose interesting photo captions or sidebars from magazine articles.
- Choose an appealing paragraph from a novel you're reading.
- Select a portion of a newspaper article, an advertisement, or even a comic strip.
- Choose some of the print in your environment, such as in a fast-food restaurant, or a supermarket, or on signs.
- Select a piece of personal writing.

Writing a Found Poem

Planning

1. Skim the print from your chosen source to find a passage or group of words that appeals to you as a possible choice for your found poem. The words should form a complete thought or unit of meaning. They could
   - stir up strong feelings
   - create a vivid image
   - suggest an interesting effect, such as being able to look at something ordinary in a new way

FOUND POETRY

Skill Focus

The use of **punctuation** and **capitalization** helps your reader to read your words and to understand the meaning of your writing.

Experiment with adding or removing punctuation to create effect and to promote meaning in your found poem. Use capitalization as another way to add emphasis to words you want to stress in your poem.

For more about punctuation and capitalization, see pages 175–180 of the Tool Kit.

Drafting

FOR MORE ABOUT THE WORDS IN BOLD, SEE THE STYLE FILE.

1 Copy the original text, arranging the text into lines and, perhaps, stanzas.
- Each line is a unit of meaning. A line may be a single word, part of a word, a phrase, or a sentence.
- Stanzas (the grouping of a number of lines) may be used to show changes in time, place, **atmosphere,** speaker, or focus.

2 Establish your own **voice** for the poem by experimenting with different arrangements for line length, **rhythm,** and emphasis.
- Control the way your poem will be read by grouping together certain ideas or images in different line lengths and stanzas.
- Squeezing together, spacing out, or separating a word within a line creates an emphasis in the arrangement and meaning of the poem.
- Letters that are spaced out, condensed, or placed higher or lower than others in the line gets more emphasis. For example, spaced-out letters indicate that readers should stretch out the word as they read it.

3 Add or remove punctuation and capitalization to create the meaning and feeling you want for your poem. Ellipses (…) may be used to show where words have been cut from the original text. (For more about punctuation and capitalization, see the Skill Focus.)

4 Cite the original text source, if applicable, by stating the name of the publication and the date published; or the title of a book, the author's name, and the page number.

5 Decide if you will use the title of the original text or create your own title.

Revising

Read your poem aloud to yourself or with a partner. Consider these suggestions.

- Is your poem a complete thought?
- Does your found poem create a new awareness or emphasis for the original text?
- Do you need to rearrange any words, letters, or lines for a better effect? Are specific words and images emphasized?
- Have you used stanzas?
- Have you created your own voice, different from the original source?
- Have you used punctuation and capitalization to help your readers understand your meaning?

Editing

FOR MORE ABOUT THE WORDS IN BOLD, SEE THE TOOL KIT.

Check your writing for

- **punctuation** and **capitalization**
- proper use of **ellipsis**
- correct **spelling**

Publishing

- Make a small number of computer printouts of your poem and give them to friends or family members.
- Perform a dramatic reading of your found poem for your classmates.
- Submit your found poem to your school newspaper or newsletter.

Reflecting

- What is the most challenging aspect of creating a found poem?
- How did you solve problems with arranging your poem on the page?
- What advice would you offer to others about writing found poetry?

COMPUTER LINK

Arranging your found poem on computer makes it easier to experiment with moving your text and with emphasizing different words for different effects. You can experiment until you find the perfect arrangement for your poem.

Instructions

- **Rules**

Instructions are useful pieces of writing. They guide you through a process by providing a sequenced series of actions or steps. If you doubt the importance of well-written instructions, just imagine trying to tie your shoelaces for the first time without someone showing you how.

Better yet, try writing instructions to tell someone how to tie shoelaces. To make it really challenging, pretend this someone is an alien who doesn't even know what shoes are! If you actually try this exercise (perhaps just imagining it will work), you'll appreciate how important it is for written instructions to be clear, concise, and logically ordered or arranged.

Rules

Some people think life has too many rules, but can you imagine what life would be like without them? Rules aren't always written down, but they are understood and apply to all aspects of our lives. Rules for behaving in an acceptable manner and for working with others are a big part of our lives—they help us to work things out fairly.

Organized groups and clubs, such as your school's student council or drama club, or a youth group in your community, use rules to set limits and expectations for members. Rules often show consideration for different age or skill groups and safely provide for these groups.

Every organized sport has rules, whether it's the minor sports program in your community or the professional sports organizations of Major League Baseball or the National Hockey League. While the playing area may be different, board games and other stationary games share the need for rules with active games. Rules for these games and sports tell players what is allowed and how to finish and win the game.

Contests that offer awards and prizes also need rules to tell you how you may enter and win. These rules are an agreement or a contract between you and the contest-holder to do something in a certain way.

Writing rules will help you gain a better understanding of how and why rules are made.

Writing Goals

As you develop your rules, ensure that you

- identify and model the features of rules
- sequence your text in a logical order
- keep the information clear and concise
- use short command sentences

Set one or two additional writing goals (skills you want to work on) for yourself.

Have you ever seen any rules like these ones written by Rashad?

title clearly identifies the rules

Pool Rules

1. Children under the age of 10 must be accompanied by an adult.
2. No street clothes allowed in pool area.
3. Shower before entering the pool area.
4. No more than 15 people allowed in the pool at a time.
5. No flotation devices allowed in the pool.
6. No running on the pool deck.

may be written as positive or negative statements

short command sentences

Study Rules

Establishing and following some simple study rules can help you to become a better student.

an introduction states the purpose

ESTABLISH A HOMEWORK ROUTINE
1. Choose a quiet place to do your homework.
2. Try to do your work at the same time every day.

KEEP TRACK OF ASSIGNMENTS
1. Carry an assignment notebook with you all the time.
2. Write down every assignment with its due date. Jot down any other special information such as length or format.
3. Write your assignments on a monthly calendar.
4. Highlight the long-range assignments like a research report using a symbol or highlighting marker.

headings organize information into smaller groupings

CREATE A SCHEDULE
1. Develop a study schedule for tests that shows when and what you'll study.
2. Use a schedule to help you plan for long-range assignments. Remember to leave time for revising and editing your work.

rules are numbered in order of importance

Features of Rules

- Rules
  - have a title
  - may have an introduction that states the purpose of the rules
  - follow a logical sequence and are generally numbered
  - are often organized under different headings
  - are written using short command sentences or point form
- Rules may be written in positive or negative statements.

  POSITIVE *Play will stop when the puck goes over the boards.*
  NEGATIVE *Do not shoot the puck over the boards.*

- The language may be formal or informal.
- Brief descriptions may be included to clarify or support rules.
- Illustrations, diagrams, or photographs may be included along with the text.

Choose an Idea

- Write the rules you use to play your favourite card game. Revise the rules to include more players, or to change the value of the cards, or create different rules for winning the game.
- Write the rules for being a good citizen in the twenty-first century.
- What are the rules for using public transit (bus, ferry, train, subway)? Choose one type of transit and write the rules.
- Develop a contest for your classroom or school and write the rules for entering and winning.
- Write house rules for living in your home.
- Write rules for being a good friend.

Check These Out!

Reading a variety of different types of rules can help you write your own. Look at the rules posted in your community, and the rules for your favourite game. Check out the rules associated with contests advertised in magazines, in junk mail, and on cereal boxes. Have you seen either of these books?

- *The Game Treasury* by Merilyn Symonds Mohr
- *Card Games Around the World* by Sid Jackson

Writing Rules

Planning

FOR MORE ABOUT THE WORD IN BOLD, SEE THE STYLE FILE.

1. Brainstorm a list of possible topics for your rules. Think about who will use these rules and what kinds of information they will need to know.
2. Decide if you will include an introduction to your rules. You might give some background information or choose to highlight the benefits or rewards of following the rules. You may also include information about eligibility or special conditions.
3. Think about the **tone** of your rules. Will you write them in a formal, serious tone or will they be informal and perhaps even humorous?

Drafting

1. Write a title for your rules to explain their purpose.
2. Write your introduction to match the purpose of your rules. For example, an introduction to contest rules pulls in readers with an offer to win prizes, while an introduction to school rules may emphasize safety and cooperation.
3. Decide whether you will write your rules using positive or negative statements, or a mixture of both.
4. Jot down rules for each of the topics you have brainstormed. Keep the rules simple and easy to follow. Include only one main point in each rule.
5. When writing your rules, use accurate nouns to tell the reader specifically what you are talking about and use action verbs in the present tense; for example, "Choose a quiet place to study."
6. Use short command sentences. (See the Skill Focus.)

Skill Focus

Command sentences speak directly to the reader and give an order or direction. They usually begin with a verb in the present tense, and end with a period.
For example:
Allow passengers to exit the subway train before entering.

For more about sentences, see page 167 of the Tool Kit.

7 Organize your rules into a logical sequence to make it easy for your readers to understand them. You might begin with general rules and move to specific ones, or begin with the most important rule and end with the least important. Will you number your rules to show their importance?

8 Decide if organizing your rules into smaller groups with headings would make them easier to understand.

9 Consider adding illustrations or diagrams to support your rules.

Revising

Once your first draft is written, work with a classmate to revise your rules. Consider these suggestions.

- Does your introduction match the purpose of your rules?
- Is the purpose of your rules clearly stated?
- Did you include all of the important rules?
- Are your rules in a logical order, such as in order of importance?
- Have you numbered the rules or organized them under headings?
- Do you need to add any missing information or to rearrange the order of the rules?
- Have you used short, tight command sentences that speak directly to the reader?
- Can you cut any unnecessary words or information to make your rules easier to understand?
- Have you been consistent with the tone of your rules, whether it is formal or informal?
- Do illustrations, diagrams, or photographs support the rules and make them easier to understand?

COMPUTER LINK

If you decide to publish your rules, you might design them on the computer for a more professional look. Choose an interesting but readable typeface for the text. Experiment with ways to make your headings stand out.

Editing

FOR MORE ABOUT THE WORDS IN BOLD, SEE THE TOOL KIT.

Check your writing for
- clear and complete **sentences**
- accurate **nouns** and active **verbs**
- correct **spelling**

Publishing

- Invite a partner or small group to play your favourite card game according to your revised rules. Try the game at home.
- Share your rules for being a good citizen in the twenty-first century by posting them on a classroom bulletin-board display.
- Collect all the rules written by the class for using public transit and publish them in a book. Send a copy of the book to your local transit authority.
- Run your contest by publishing the contest rules in your classroom or school newspaper.
- Share your household rules with your family. Use your rules as the basis for a "family contract" that outlines such things as who does what chores, what the privileges are, and so on.
- Put together a class anthology of rules for being a good friend.

Reflecting

- How do you think rules should be established? Who should make them and when should they be changed?
- What are the three most important rules you live by?
- How did writing rules help you to understand how and why rules are made?

Drama

- ## Reader's Theatre Scripts

"All the world's a stage" or at least that's what William Shakespeare said. He may have overstated it a bit, but drama does play a large role in our lives. When we watch television shows, movies, or plays, it's often difficult to remember that they all started out as scripts.

A script tells a story and uses the same elements as other forms of narrative—characters, plot, and setting—but a script breaks everything down a little further by indicating characters or narrators and assigning them spoken words. Scripts also include extra information such as stage directions. These extras help the director and actors turn a script into a dramatic experience for the audience to enjoy.

Reader's Theatre Scripts

If you'd like to see a piece of writing dramatically presented, turn it into a reader's theatre script. Scripts can be based on any type of writing format, including poetry, novels, plays, short stories, diaries, letters, or even essays. Each performer assumes the role of a character or narrator and, in turn, reads aloud to an audience. Performers use only their voices and body language to show how the characters think, feel, and act, and to reveal all of the action of the piece.

Performers often stand or sit in a line to read reader's theatre scripts directly to the audience. Props are kept to a minimum as the focus is on the way the performers dramatize the text.

So choose your favourite poem or the most exciting part of the novel you're reading and turn it into a dynamic, dramatic reader's theatre script.

Writing Goals

As you develop your reader's theatre script, ensure that you

- identify and model the features of reader's theatre scripts
- choose a text appropriate for scripting
- determine the number of voices or performers needed
- use proper punctuation to make your meaning clear

Set one or two additional writing goals (skills you want to work on) for yourself.

Andrea turned her mystery short story into a reader's theatre script. Here is an excerpt from her script.

The Scent of Murder

Characters:
- Detective Tim Shields
- Police Chief O'Hara
- Rosie Peterson
- Narrator 2
- Mary Gale
- Myra Tams
- Narrator 1

Narrator 1: Tim Shields received the call at nine in the morning—an apparent suicide according to his old friend Chief O'Hara. He stuffed his bag with the usual: notebook, cell phone, and an apple in case he got hungry. Then he rushed over to Parkglen Drive, to the home of Mr. and Mrs. Gale.

Chief O'Hara: It's not suicide Shields. The gun was placed in the opposite direction in the hand. He couldn't have shot himself with the gun in his hand the way it was. Obviously an amateur. Here's the note.

Narrator 2: O'Hara handed him a white sheet of paper encased in a slim plastic bag.

Tim Shields: *(reading)* "Good-bye dreadful life." Well, let's hear what Mrs. Gale has to say.

Narrator 1: A chalk outline of a body, Mr. Gale's, Shields presumed, was drawn on the tile floor of the kitchen. In the corner of the room, there was a woman crying profusely. Another younger woman was trying to comfort her with soothing words. She stopped and looked at him as he entered the room.

Shields: Mind if I ask you some questions?

Narrator 2: The woman who had been crying got up and quickly left the room. The other woman spoke up.

Myra Tams: *(softly)* I don't mind.

Shields: And you are?

Myra: Myra Tams. I'm Mrs. Gale's personal assistant.

Shields: Are you the one who found the body?

Myra: Oh no. I came from picking up the dry cleaning to find all of these police officers and poor Mrs. Gale. She was in a terrible state when I got here.

Narrator 1: She sobbed a little as she spoke.

Shields: Then it was Mrs. Gale who found the body? What is her first name?

Myra: It's Mary-Ann but she prefers to be called Mary. Yes, I believe she did find the body—Mr. Gale, I mean.

Shields: Did Mr. Gale have any enemies that you know of, Ms. Tams?

Myra: Well…

- list of all characters and narrators
- the name of the character or narrator is on the left side of the page
- spoken words are on the right side of the page
- directions to the reader are in parentheses
- characters read dialogue
- narrators read unspoken thoughts, narration, and action

READER'S THEATRE SCRIPTS

Features of Reader's Theatre Scripts

Check These Out!

Examining reader's theatre scripts and books about performing a reader's theatre can help you write your own. Check out the following.
- *Reader's Theatre Anthology* by Mel White
- *Reader's Theatre for Young Adults* by Kathy Latrobe
- *Learning with Reader's Theatre* by Neill Dixon

- A reader's theatre script retells text (a story, poem, report, letter) through dialogue and narration.
- All characters and narrators are listed at the beginning of the script.
- The names of the characters and narrators appear on the left side of the page and their spoken words on the right.
- Each character is assigned all of the dialogue for that character from the original narrative.
- The narrators are assigned all the text from the original narrative that is not dialogue—actions, narration, and unspoken thoughts.
- The amount of text is distributed evenly. Several narrators can break up large chunks of text.
- The length of a reader's theatre may vary from one minute to twenty minutes in length.

Choose an Idea

- Create a reader's theatre script to present a report. Make sure your teacher has a copy to follow as you perform.
- Rewrite a story you have written as a reader's theatre script.
- Choose a humorous or suspenseful scene from a novel and script it for a reader's theatre presentation. Be sure to select a scene with plenty of dialogue.
- Take an interesting topic of history that you've learned in social studies and write an original reader's theatre script. You may have to research the characters you are portraying.
- Do you have a favourite poem? Write it in script format.

Writing a Reader's Theatre Script

Planning

FOR MORE ABOUT THE WORDS IN BOLD, SEE THE STYLE FILE.

1. Think about your audience, purpose, and performance—will it be performed for a class presentation, a club meeting, or a school assembly?
2. Find an interesting topic to write about or choose a piece of text that would suit your audience. Is it entertaining? Brainstorm with a few people to get their opinions. Sometimes what you find interesting is not so entertaining to others.
3. Decide if the text can be easily scripted.
   - Is the vocabulary and content suitable for your audience?
   - Is there a lot of **dialogue** to suit a reader's theatre performance? Is there some **narration?** (Remember, long stretches of narration can be condensed and summarized to keep only the main points that move the plot along.) Will there be roles for several people?
   - Is the text a complete unit with a beginning and an end? This is especially important if you are using only a section of text; for example, a scene from a novel.
   - Is the **plot** simple and well paced?

COMPUTER LINK

Typing and formatting your reader's theatre script on computer will enable you to make it clear, organized, and legible. You can also print multiple copies of your script from the computer.

Drafting

FOR MORE ABOUT THE WORDS IN BOLD, SEE THE STYLE FILE.

1. Decide on the number of performers needed to present the text. If there is dialogue, you will need a different performer for each **character.** Narration can be divided among several **narrators.** Keep the amount of text balanced and evenly distributed among the performers.
2. The text for the narrators could be as it was originally written if it is a story or novel excerpt, or you could adapt and summarize the gaps between the dialogue. This might include actions, unspoken thoughts, and scenery or time changes.

Skill Focus

A **colon** is a mark of punctuation that tells a reader to "note what follows." Colons are used in scripts to indicate the dialogue or text that each speaker is to read.

For more about colons, see page 176 of the Tool Kit.

3 Characters can read the dialogue only and the narrator can add dialogue tags such as "the farmer muttered." Or this information can be left out and the characters can reveal it in role.

4 List all of the characters and the narrator at the beginning of the script. If there is more than one narrator, list them as Narrator 1, Narrator 2, and so on.

5 Performers need to see their parts quickly and easily. Write the names of each character and narrator followed by a colon on the left side of the page. Put their spoken words on the right side of the page. Keep an equal margin between the characters' names and the spoken words. (See the Skill Focus for more about colons.)

6 Type your script and provide enough copies for each performer to have one.

Revising

Once you have a draft of your script, ask a friend to read it or read it aloud to yourself and consider the following ideas.

- Is the plot simple enough to understand and is there an obvious beginning and end?
- Is it interesting enough to entertain the audience?
- Are the characters easily identifiable and different from one another? Does personality come through in the dialogue?
- Are any changes in the setting clearly stated in the narration?
- Is the dialogue and the narration balanced so that the audience will understand what is happening and who is speaking?
- If you have rewritten or condensed any narration, have you carefully chosen each word? Consider how the words and sentences will sound when read aloud.
- Does each performer have enough to say?
- Time the reading to see how long it will take and to ensure that the performance is not so long that it becomes boring. Keep it under twenty minutes in length.

Editing

FOR MORE ABOUT THE WORDS IN BOLD, SEE THE TOOL KIT.

Check your writing for
- clear, complete **sentences**
- proper **punctuation,** especially **colons**
- correct **spelling**

Publishing

- Ask the librarian to catalogue your reader's theatre script for other students to read or to perform.
- Perform your written script for the specific occasion it was written for, such as a school assembly or a class report.
- Form a reader's theatre group and perform at noon hour while students eat their lunch.
- Tape-record a dramatic reading of your script and take it home for family members to enjoy.

Reflecting

- How is writing a reader's theatre script different from other types of writing?
- What type of writing format do you think is the easiest or hardest to script?
- What advice would you give to someone who was writing a reader's theatre script?

INFO

Here are a few suggestions to help you, as the writer and director, to perform your reader's theatre.
- Make sure everyone understands the plot and the script.
- Rehearse until all of the performers are comfortable with their roles.
- Help performers use their voices and body language to reflect their character's personality, feelings, and actions.
- Props, if any are used, should be simple, as the focus is on the performers' interpretation of the text they are reading.

Persuasive

- ***Letters to the Editor***
- ***Speeches***

Is there an issue or topic that you have strong feelings about, or do you want to share some information that you think others might be interested in? If the answer to these questions is yes, persuasive writing could be just what you need.

Persuasive writing tries to convince others to accept, or at least to consider, your point of view. Delivering a well-thought-out argument to a specific audience—whether by a letter to the editor, a persuasive essay, an editorial, or a speech—might be enough to convince others to change their minds, or to take action for a cause or issue that you think is important.

Letters to the Editor

Do you have strong opinions about issues affecting your life and the world around you? Do you wish you had a means to express your opinions to other people who might be persuaded to your way of thinking? One way to have your voice heard is to express yourself and your opinions in a letter to the editor of a newspaper or magazine.

Writing a letter to the editor is something that many people do when they feel strongly about an issue and want to reach a large audience. These letters are often written to raise people's awareness of an issue or problem, or to persuade the reader to take some action. Some letters to the editor are written in reaction to an editorial, an article, or even to another letter to the editor.

People your age can have a strong voice when it comes to speaking out about the many issues that concern you. Take the opportunity to share a persuasive argument with a large group of people who may not have considered your point of view before—write a letter to the editor.

Writing Goals

As you develop your letter to the editor, ensure that you

- identify and model the features of letters to the editor
- think of a topic or issue that you feel strongly about
- use jot notes or an outline to build a convincing argument
- use correct spelling and punctuation in your final draft

Set one or two additional writing goals (skills you want to work on) for yourself.

May wrote a letter to the editor expressing her concerns about the pollution at her local beach.

May Appleby
12 Blaine Way
Hamilton, ON
L8N 1Z5

December 2, 1997

Editor
Hamilton Spectator
44 Frid Street
Hamilton, ON
L8N 3G3

salutation → Dear Sir or Madam:

first-person point of view → I am writing to express my concerns about pollution in the waters of Singing Sands Beach. ← **body of the letter**

opinion → Pollution is dangerous to both the wildlife and people who use the beach. Chemicals such as copper, lead, and chlorine are dumped by industries. These chemicals reach the lake and contaminate the water, affecting the fish and their food supply. The chemical-filled water is just as dangerous to the people who use the beach. We're afraid to even step in the water—not to mention the smell. People living near the beach have to keep their doors and windows closed because of the odour. ← **facts to support the argument**

It will take all our combined efforts to make the beach a safe place to swim. We could get a group of people from the community together to clean up the beach and plant more trees. But we need Environment Canada's support to help us find out where the pollution is coming from, to stop further dumping, and to clean up the lake and beach. I urge the government to take our concerns to heart. We need to make our environment safe for future generations.

closing → Sincerely,

May Appleby ← **signature**

May Appleby

PERSUASIVE

Features of Letters to the Editor

- A letter to the editor
  - expresses an opinion and raises people's consciousness about an issue or problem
  - can be written as a response to an editorial, another letter, a column, or an article
  - follows a standard letter format with a salutation (greeting), body, closing, and signature
  - clearly states an opinion and offers details and facts to support the opinion and to build a convincing argument
  - is usually written from a first-person point of view, using pronouns such as "I" and "we."

Check These Out!

Reading letters to the editor will help you get ideas for writing and setting up your own. Look in your local newspaper and in a variety of magazines.

Choose an Idea

- Write a letter to the editor of your local newspaper about an issue affecting your community.
- Write a humorous letter to the editor. For example, write from the point of view of your cat complaining about the quality of kitty litter today.
- Write a response to an article or to a letter to the editor in a magazine you enjoy.
- Use the information you've researched for a science or social studies report, and write a letter to the editor expressing your opinion about it.
- Create a classroom "issues" magazine. Include letters to the editor about issues that affect you and your friends.

INFO

If your letter to the editor gets published, don't be surprised if it looks different. Your printed letter may have been edited for clarity or length, and it might appear with a headline.

If you keep your letter brief and to the point you have a better chance of it appearing the way you wrote it.

Check the letters page of the newspaper or magazine for guidelines and the address for where to send your letter.

Writing a Letter to the Editor

Planning

1 Decide what issue or topic you feel strongly about. Jot down a few ideas and choose the best one.

2. Think about your audience. Who are you trying to persuade with your letter to the editor? Classmates? People in your community?

3. What information will you need to express your opinion? Will you need to conduct research to find facts? (For more about conducting research, see pages 154–159 of the Tool Kit.)

4. Organize your information. Write your opinion and then list several facts to support it. For every fact, try to list a few good examples. This combination of your opinion, facts, and examples forms your argument.

Drafting

FOR MORE ABOUT THE WORDS IN BOLD, SEE THE STYLE FILE.

1. Develop your argument into an interesting **lead** (opening paragraph). The lead should clearly state what your letter to the editor will try to convince readers about. Explain the problem or situation and then state your opinion.

2. Write paragraphs supporting the argument you've expressed in your lead. Develop your ideas logically using facts and related examples in each paragraph.

3. Be polite. Don't get carried away, even though you may feel strongly about the issue.

4. Write from a first-person **point of view,** using pronouns such as "I" and "we." (See the Skill Focus for more about point of view.)

5. Wrap up your letter to the editor with a thoughtful or persuasive summary of your opinion on the issue. Suggest ways to improve or change the situation. Your comments should be strong enough to change your readers' minds, or at least to help them see the situation from another viewpoint.

Skill Focus

The **point of view** is the angle from which your letter is written. When you are writing in the first person, you are writing from your own point of view to express your own opinions. You will be using pronouns such as "I," "we," "my," "me," and "mine."

If you are writing to respond to what someone else has written, you would use the third-person point of view as well, using pronouns such as "she," "he," or "they."

For more about point of view, first person, and third person, see page 146 of the Style File.

Revising

Once you have a draft of your letter to the editor, consider these questions.

- Read your letter to the editor out loud. Does it make sense? Is it well organized?
- Is your opinion clearly stated?
- Have you included facts and examples to support your opinion? Have you checked the accuracy of your facts and dates?
- Ask friends or family members to read your letter. Do they find your argument convincing?
- Have you met the guidelines of the magazine or newspaper for the acceptable number of words?
- Have you included your full name, address, and telephone number?

Editing

FOR MORE ABOUT THE WORDS IN BOLD, SEE THE TOOL KIT.

Check your writing for

- **sentence** variety
- proper **capitalization** and **punctuation**
- correct **spelling**

Publishing

- Send your letter to the editor of your local newspaper.
- Read your letter to the editor to your class or to another class.
- Publish your classroom "issues" magazine. Share your publication with family, friends, and people in the community.
- If you wrote a humorous letter, submit it to the editor of your class newsletter or post it on a bulletin-board display.

COMPUTER LINK

You could send your letter to the editor by e-mail. Most publications list an Internet address, along with their postal address, on the letters page.

Reflecting

- What new writing techniques did you learn?
- What do you think you can accomplish by writing a letter to the editor?

Speeches

Are you looking for a way to have your ideas heard? Do you want to persuade someone to look at an issue from your point of view? Or perhaps you want to inform people about a topic you think they'd find interesting. A good speech can be all these things—entertaining, informative, and persuasive.

Speeches can be such powerful, persuasive, and inspirational tools, and some have helped to change history. Martin Luther King's famous "I have a dream" speech, for example, opened people's eyes to social injustice and inspired them to try to make their country a better place.

Writing Goals

As you develop your speech, ensure that you

- identify and model the features of speeches
- use an outline to develop and organize your argument
- include "narrative hooks" such as famous quotations, anecdotes, and jokes
- experiment with sentence lengths and style, and punctuation

Set one or two additional writing goals (skills you want to work on) for yourself.

Examine this excerpt of the speech Joel wrote for his school's speech competition.

a surprising comment grabs the listeners' attention	I am a businessman. I make tough decisions, plan for the future, and try to make my customers happy. Now, you won't find my company in the "Fortune 500" or even in the Yellow Pages. You see, I am the co-owner of J and J Lawn Service of Bothwell, Ontario.

main argument is clearly stated at the beginning

Chairperson, honourable judges, and friends: to the unfamiliar it's just grass but to my brother and me it's growing money. Since 1994 Jordan and I have been cutting grass, raking and bagging leaves, cleaning flower beds and the like for some of the most wonderful people on the face of the earth.

a metaphor compares grass to growing money

Our many experiences in the tough world of business have taught us many valuable lessons about life and about ourselves.

facts and reasons support the main argument

I don't want this to sound like an infomercial, but my brother and I do pretty good work. I've seen a lot of those professional landscapers around with their hi-tech, heavy duty machines. You know the kind, they have the biggest and most expensive equipment on the market. They charge their customers an arm and a leg and I don't think they do as good a job as we do. From this I've learned that bigger is not always better.

using your own words makes the speech sound natural when it is presented

Our equipment is pretty fair. We have a John Deere STX 38 garden tractor and a lawn sweeper for raking up grass clippings and leaves. We have a home-made wooden trailer that carries our push mower and smaller equipment. Once, when we were cutting on the other side of town, the draw pin that holds our trailer onto the tractor got lost. It looked like we were in an impossible situation until we managed to find a stick to replace the pin and we were able to pull everything home in one piece. You see we've learned to become very resourceful at times.

emotional language is used to persuade the audience

Now, Jordan and I are brothers so we don't always get along. There has been the odd argument on the job that has sometimes led to labour unrest. One sticky summer day Jordan and I were stuck in a backyard pulling weeds. It got to the point where Jordan said he couldn't take it anymore. He sat and wouldn't work. Noticing that I was now doing all of the work, I went on strike. Negotiations lasted several minutes until we both agreed to return to the job. From the incident I learned that working with a partner is not always easy.

anecdotes are one type of "narrative hook" used for effect and to add interest

SPEECHES

Check These Out!

Listen to speeches on television and radio for ideas on how to write and present a convincing speech. Also see
- *Great Speeches in History* (3 volumes) by William Safire
- *Classic Speeches* edited by Richard Crosscup
- *How to Make Speeches for all Occasions* by Harold P. Zelco and Marjorie E. Zelco
- *Speak Up With Confidence* by Jack Valenti

Features of Speeches

- A speech is spoken, but it is written first.
- A main argument or opinion is clearly stated at the beginning.
- The body of the speech tries to convince the listener.
- The main argument is supported by reasons and supporting facts.
- The opposite viewpoint is sometimes mentioned to point out its weaknesses and to show that the speaker has considered all viewpoints.
- Jokes, stories, anecdotes, famous quotations, song lyrics, or excerpts from literature may be used for added effect and to interest the audience.
- Speeches use emotional language to excite, inform, or persuade the audience.

Choose an Idea

- Write a speech about an issue that you care about or would like to learn more about. The issue might be environmental, global, or social.
- Write a speech about a famous person in history; for example, Terry Fox or Madame Curie.
- Write a speech about a topic that interests you, such as the role of technology in the classroom.
- Write a speech that a famous politician or historical figure might give to an audience. Be sure to check your facts so that your information is correct.
- Write a speech that you would give if you were running for the student council at your school or for the leader of your youth group.

Writing a Speech

Planning

FOR MORE ABOUT THE WORDS IN BOLD, SEE THE STYLE FILE.

1 Choose an issue or topic that would make an interesting speech. Narrow the focus of your issue or topic. It is easier to deal with a small part of a larger issue.

PERSUASIVE

2 Think about your audience and your purpose. Do you want to persuade, to entertain, to explain, or to inform? Or do you want to accomplish all of these goals?
- How large is your audience? A speech written in **informal language** may be more appropriate for a smaller group.
- What age is your audience? If your speech is for younger students, you'll have to keep it short. You might also consider using music, puppets, or props to make it more interesting for younger children.

3 Once you know your topic and audience, it's time to gather your information. List the questions you want answers to and gather information from all the available sources. Make notes on any important or interesting information that you find. (For more about conducting research, see pages 154–159 of the Tool Kit.)

4 Organize your information by choosing five or six main points to talk about. Then write an outline by listing points (accurate facts and clear examples) for each main point.

Speech Outline

TOPIC - what I've learned about business
OPINION - making money can be hard work and working for myself means being responsible

POINT 1 - I'm a businessman.
- co-owner of business
- make decisions and plan for the future

POINT 2 - Bigger isn't always better.
- we do good work.
- professional landscapers charge a lot of money but we do a better job

POINT 3 - We're resourceful.
- have our own equipment
- tell about when we lost the pin to hold the trailer on

> POINT 4 - Working with a partner isn't always easy.
> - we have some problems
> - we have the odd argument but we work it out
> - tell about when Jordan stopped working and I went on strike
>
> POINT 5 - Advertising helps to make a business successful.
> - for the last three summers we have joined the parade
> - small float and decorate tractor
> - tell about the high winds last year
>
> CONCLUSION
> - I've learned that making money can be very hard work
> - I have to be responsible
> - hopefully I can put everything I've learned about business to good use in the future

Skill Focus

Use comparisons in your writing to clarify any information that may not be clear and to spice up your speech. **Metaphors** and **similes** can spark the imagination of your audience by describing a person, place, or thing by comparing it to something else.

Metaphors make a direct comparison while similes use the words "like" or "as."

METAPHOR

Wild thoughts are express trains in my head.

SIMILE

*Wild thoughts shoot through my head **like** an express train.*

For more about metaphors and similes, see pages 143 and 150 of the Style File.

Drafting

FOR MORE ABOUT THE WORDS IN BOLD, SEE THE STYLE FILE.

1. Write an exciting introduction to your speech. Writing the introduction first will help you to focus on what you are going to say and how you are going to say it. You could begin by asking an interesting question, telling a famous quotation or a funny story, or making a surprising or unusual comment. Your introduction should grab your listener's attention and clearly state your argument or opinion.
2. Now use your outline to help you plan what you're going to say in the body of your speech.
   - Add facts and examples to the outline that will help your audience understand your points and to convince them of your viewpoint. You can use **anecdotes, similes** and **metaphors,** and details about *who, what, where, when, why,* and *how.* (See the Skill Focus for more about similes and metaphors.)
   - Use your own words so your speech will sound natural when you present it.

PERSUASIVE

3 Write your conclusion. Recall the main points you have made and end with a line that sums up your main argument, or encourages your audience to take action.
4 Look for sections in your speech where you can use visuals or audio segments. Visuals can include charts, diagrams, maps, photographs, or posters. Audio can include music, sound effects, or the sound portion of a video.

Revising

As you revise your speech, consider the following suggestions.

- Read your speech to classmates or family members. Do they find it convincing?
- Does your speech make sense? Is it well organized?
- Have you used an interesting or exciting opening to grab your listener's attention?
- Have you stated your argument clearly in the introduction?
- Have you included facts and examples to support your argument?
- Does your conclusion sum up the main points?
- Have you thought about the questions your audience might ask? Make sure you have included information to answer these questions.
- Time your speech to make sure you have enough material for the time you have been given.
- Have you used a variety of sentence styles and proper punctuation for clarity? (See the Skill Focus.)

Editing

FOR MORE ABOUT THE WORDS IN BOLD, SEE THE TOOL KIT.

Check your writing for

- **sentence variety**
- well-developed **paragraphs**
- proper **punctuation** and **spelling**

Skill Focus

When revising your speech, ensure that the **punctuation** helps to clarify meaning and look at your **sentence styles** and lengths. Read your speech out loud. If you stumble over a word, a sentence, or punctuation, revise it to make it easier to read.

Avoid overly long sentences because they are difficult to read. Use commas properly in longer sentences so that you will know when to pause. Vary the style of your sentences by asking a question and then answering it, by following a long sentence with a short one, and by inverting some sentences.

For more about sentences and punctuation, see pages 167–171 and 175–180 of the Tool Kit.

INFO

Here are a few suggestions to help you present the best speech that you can.

BEFORE YOUR SPEECH

- Make cue cards. Use a separate recipe card for each main point.
- Highlight words that you want to emphasize as you speak.
- Memorize your opening line and your conclusion.
- Practise giving your speech in front of a mirror.
- Tape-record your speech and then listen to it.

DURING YOUR SPEECH

- Make eye contact with your audience.
- Speak loudly enough to be heard clearly.
- Be sure that you appear relaxed in the way you are standing or sitting while presenting your speech.
- If you are giving a formal speech, dress for the part.
- Smile!

Publishing

- Present your speech to an audience.
- Publish your speech in a class collection of speeches.
- If your speech is about an issue, send a copy to someone involved in the issue; for example, the head of an organization or your Member of Parliament.
- Present your speech on a local television or radio program, if possible.
- Videotape or audiotape your speech and choose appropriate music and sound effects for the background.

Reflecting

- What new techniques did you learn from writing a speech?
- What did you learn about developing an argument and giving an opinion?
- What advice would you give to someone who is writing and presenting a speech?
- Does it make a difference to write a speech for different audiences? Which age groups do you like to speak to? Why?

Style File

The Style File is a glossary of writing terms and techniques: the terms are listed alphabetically, with definitions and suggestions for how to use them in your writing. Knowing when and how to use different writing techniques can help you become a better writer. To get to know the Style File, flip through it and read the headings. Some of the terms may be familiar to you, but read them over to see if you have the correct meaning. Other terms will be new, so read the ones that sound intriguing or spark your interest. Keep in mind that some techniques are more suited to one format than another. For example, foreshadowing is a technique you would use when writing narrative, especially mysteries, but alliteration and rhyme are more often used in poetry and commercials.

The next time you are writing or revising a piece of writing, refer to the Style File to see if there are any techniques you could use. Gradually you'll get to know exactly what's in the Style File and be able to use many of the techniques it describes.

ACTION

The **action** is what happens in a story and involves the events or conflicts. All the actions together create the plot of a story. There are many techniques you can use to move the action along.

- Describe what is happening by writing descriptive and narrative paragraphs that reveal the events. Add details to help your reader picture the scene.
- Use dialogue to reveal things that have happened or are happening. Dialogue between characters can quickly reveal the events in your story.

ALLITERATION

Alliteration is the repetition of the same consonant sounds. It occurs most often at the beginning of words; for example, "**tr**ied and **tr**ue" and "**s**afe and **s**ound," but it can occur in other parts of a word as in "avai**l**able" and "a**ll**."

- Writers use alliteration to emphasize the words in which the repetition occurs, to give structure to a poem or story, and because it is pleasing to the ear. In the lines below, alliteration is used to draw attention to the eagle's and the land's human qualities.

> He **cl**asps the **cr**ag with **cr**ooked hands;
> **Cl**ose to the sun in **l**onely **l**ands,
> from *The Eagle* by Alfred, Lord Tennyson

- Alliteration is also used to catch the reader's attention in advertising.
- Beware, too much alliteration can distract your reader.

ANECDOTE

An **anecdote** is a brief story that shares an interesting or amusing event. Anecdotes can be used to make a point and can add spice or interest to many types of writing.

- You can use anecdotes to introduce a speech, or in a memoir, diary, commercial, autobiography, or biography.
- Description and dialogue are used to bring the event alive for the reader.

ANTAGONIST

The **antagonist** is the person or thing in a story fighting against the main character. Lex Luthor, for example, is the antagonist in *Superman*.

- The antagonist does not have to be a person; it could be an animal, the weather, fate, or some other condition working against the main character.
- Good writers use the antagonist to create problems for the main character and to move the plot along.

ATMOSPHERE

The **atmosphere** is the feeling created in a piece of writing through descriptive words. All writing, particularly stories and poetry, has a certain atmosphere—a feeling it gives the reader. The atmosphere may be dark and serious, or light and comic. It may change throughout the piece of writing as events unfold.

- An atmosphere of suspense is created through foreshadowing. In this opening sentence of a story, it is created through the description of the storm. You expect that something mysterious and dangerous is about to happen.

  Lightning flashed, and the wind whipped the tree branches around as if they were ribbons on a kite.

- Another word for atmosphere is **mood.**

CAPTIONS

A **caption** is a phrase or sentence that identifies or briefly explains a photograph or illustration.

- Captions are usually written above, below, or beside the image.
- If there are two images on a page, you can write one caption for both. Identify the images by their placement on the page; for example, above left; below right; top left; and so on.

CHARACTER

A **character** is a person in a narrative (a script, story, or poem). The characters you choose and how you describe them are important elements in any narrative.

- The main character (protagonist) should interest your audience. If your audience is not intrigued by your main character, they'll lose interest in reading your story. They should care what happens to the main character and want to find out how the story will turn out.
- The antagonist is the person or thing working against the protagonist. Readers should dislike the antagonist and hope that he or she doesn't win.

STYLE FILE

- Often characters have what is called a tragic flaw. Something in their personality leads to their downfall. For example, in the myth of Daedalus and Icarus, Daedalus's tragic flaw was pride. It led to his punishment by the gods.

See **characterization** for ideas on how to reveal characters.
See **antagonist** and **protagonist**.

CHARACTERIZATION

Characterization is the method or technique that writers use to reveal or describe characters and their personalities.

- Characters are revealed through a description of their physical characteristics and how they dress.
- What other characters say about them is also an effective way to reveal details. An exchange of dialogue between other characters can help to reveal a character's traits.
- Characters can also reveal themselves through their own words. Dialogue can be used to show what they are thinking and what they are feeling.
- Your characters' actions can show who they are. As your characters act in certain ways, their actions will reveal what kinds of people they are.

CLIFF-HANGER

A **cliff-hanger** is a writing technique used in all types of narrative. The writer breaks off the story at an exciting point and leaves the reader guessing about what is going to happen next.

- Cliff-hangers can be used at the end of chapters to create suspense. For example, in a mystery story, you might end a chapter with the lines,

    Irene knew who the thief was. The question now was how to prove it.

    Breaking off the action at this point leaves readers wondering what they missed, how the character figured out the mystery, and what will happen next.

- Cliff-hangers are an effective and often-used technique in radio and TV dramas. The show ends at an exciting point, leaving the audience to wonder and wait until the next episode to find out what will happen.

CONCLUSION

The **conclusion** is the end of an article or essay where you summarize your ideas. In a story, it's where all the problems are solved.

- Sum up the main ideas you have covered in your essay or article.
- Leave your audience with something to think about. You can ask an interesting question or challenge your reader to take some kind of action.
- Conclusions are an important part of speeches. It is always a good idea to sum up the main points you have covered and end with something memorable.
- Another word for conclusion is **summary.**

See **plot (resolution).**

CONFLICT

The **conflict** is the problem or struggle in a story that the characters have to overcome. The conflict also helps to start the action. There are five basic types of conflict.

1 **Person vs. person.** In this kind of conflict, a character has a problem with one or more of the other characters.
2 **Person vs. society.** A character, usually the main character, has a problem with society. It could involve a problem in school, a problem with the traditional way of doing things, or a problem with the community.
3 **Person vs. nature.** A character has a problem with something in nature: an earthquake, a snowstorm, or getting lost in the wilderness.
4 **Person vs. self.** A character goes through a personal struggle and has to decide what to do about a problem. In *Anne of Green Gables*, for example, Anne worries that her new family will not keep her.
5 **Person vs. fate.** A character fights against a problem that seems too big to control. In *Romeo and Juliet*, for example, a larger force seems to be at work against the main characters. No matter what their actions are, they seem fated to fail.

Many writers choose to use more than one conflict in their stories, which can create an exciting plot. However, keep in mind that too much happening in one story can be confusing for your reader.

DIALOGUE

Dialogue is what we call the words of a conversation when they are written down. When characters in a story or script talk to each other, it is dialogue. Writers use dialogue to show what the characters are like, what they are thinking and feeling, and what they plan to do. Dialogue can add interest to any story.

- Make it sound like the conversation you hear around you every day.
- Use words and phrases that suit the character who is speaking.
- Give your readers signals to help them understand the dialogue.
    - Every time a new character speaks, begin a new paragraph.

    "I've never been to the Calgary Stampede," Paula told her friend Karin.
    "Well, you can come with us this year," replied Karin.

    - Use dialogue or speech tags to remind the reader which character is speaking; for example:

    "When does the game start?" **Jason asked.**

    Short passages may not need dialogue tags.
    - Put the dialogue in quotation marks.
- When revising your writing, read the dialogue out loud. Does it sound natural? Does it sound as if real people are talking?

EXAGGERATION

An **exaggeration** is a statement that stretches the truth. For example, saying a person is *so tall he can see over the top of buildings* is an exaggeration. The person can be tall, but not that tall. Exaggeration is commonly used in tall tales, but it can also be effective in other types of narrative, such as scripts, commercials, and poems. Its main purpose is to add emphasis and entertainment value to your story.

- Sometimes the effect or feeling created by the exaggeration is funny, fanciful, or sad depending on the meaning and mood you are trying to create. The person in this poem excerpt, for example, will tell his or her story at a later date, and may be a little regretful about which choice he or she has made.

> *I shall be telling this with a sigh*
> *Somewhere **ages and ages hence**:*
> from "The Road Not Taken" by Robert Frost

- Another word for exaggeration is **hyperbole.**

FLASHBACK

In a **flashback,** the writer describes an earlier time in the story and explains something that will help the reader understand the plot and the characters better.

- A flashback can involve an event or a series of events, or it can explain something about a character. For example, a character could recall a time when he or she had a conversation with another character.
- Some stories have many flashbacks, but too many can confuse the reader.

FORESHADOWING

Foreshadowing is a clue or hint about what will happen later in the story. The information teases readers and keeps them guessing about what is going to happen.

- The atmosphere or mood is an important element in foreshadowing. The lights going out suddenly in a house in the dark of night, for example, can foreshadow danger.
- This technique is mainly used in mysteries to create suspense, but you can use it in other types of narrative as well. Think about how and where you can use foreshadowing in your writing.

FORMAL LANGUAGE

Formal language usually has a serious, factual, and impersonal tone. It follows conventional vocabulary and structure, and puts the reader at a distance.

- Formal language uses the third-person point of view ("he," "she," "it," "they").
- Contractions and abbreviations are not used.
- Formal language is generally used in writing that analyses or makes an argument; for example, in a persuasive essay, a research report, or a business letter.

STYLE FILE

IDIOM

An **idiom** is a common phrase or expression that means something different from what the words actually say. For example:

She got cold feet. (She changed her mind.)
It was raining cats and dogs. (It was raining heavily.)

- Idioms can add interest to your writing because they create vivid images and hold meaning beyond what the words actually say.
- While a well-chosen idiom can add a change of pace to your writing, be careful not to overuse them. Too many can become repetitive and tiresome for your reader. (An overused idiom is called a cliché.)

IMAGERY

Imagery is a technique a writer uses to create pictures in the reader's mind and to appeal to the senses of touch, taste, smell, or hearing. An image can draw a picture, strengthen a feeling, reveal characters, even create a mood, or explain an idea. The following lines of poetry have images that make readers feel they are right in the scene.

My toboggan and I carve winter
We crunch over the powdery snow
the one by one glistening grains
they sigh and squeak
from "My Toboggan and I Carve Winter" by Jane Wadley

Visual imagery is the most common form of imagery in poetry and narrative, but an image may also represent a sound, a smell, a taste, a feeling, or a sensation, such as wetness, heat, cold, hunger, or thirst. In the above poem, for example, you can almost feel and hear the crunching of the snow under the toboggan from the poet's description.

Try to create rich images in your writing that appeal to the senses.

- Use description that helps your reader to experience what you are describing. Use concrete, not vague descriptions. For example, the word "hummingbird" creates a more definite image than the word "bird." "Red-breasted hummingbird" is even more specific. Remember that imagery is created through the nouns, adjectives, verbs, and adverbs you use.
- Other writing techniques that help to create images are **similes, metaphors, personification, onomatopoeia,** and **alliteration.**

INFORMAL LANGUAGE

Informal language speaks directly to the reader in a friendly, straightforward style. It may include colloquial expressions (language that is used in everyday speech), contractions, and abbreviations. Informal language may use the first person ("I," "we," "us") and sometimes addresses the reader as "you."
You can use informal language in the following situations.

- In personal writing when you are writing for yourself; for example, in a journal.
- In messages when you know your audience well: for example, in a friendly letter, thank-you note, or memo.
- In persuasive writing when you want to develop a feeling of goodwill with your audience and appeal to their emotions; for example, a speech or a letter to the editor.
- In instructional writing when you are explaining something; for example, in rules or guides.

Note: Slang is also considered informal language, but use it sparingly.

IRONY

Irony is using a word or phrase to mean the exact opposite of its normal meaning. The most common kinds of irony are dramatic and verbal.

- In **dramatic irony,** the reader or audience knows about an event or situation that the character does not. For example, a character may say, *This is the happiest day of my life,* while members of the audience or other characters know that his house has just burned down.
- In **verbal irony,** the speaker says one thing but means something else. Both the speaker and the listener are aware of the contrast. For example, *I had a wonderful time at the party* means a boring time at the party. The listener must know the party was boring to understand the irony in the speaker's "wonderful."
- Irony is a powerful tool for you to use as a writer because it helps you to suggest meaning without stating it outright.
- When you write stories, try to use ironic statements or situations sparingly. If you use irony only once in a while, it will have a greater effect.

Note: Be careful how you use irony. If not written properly, your reader may get the opposite meaning to what you intended.

STYLE FILE

JARGON

Jargon refers to the specialized words or terminology used in certain situations and occupations. Every occupation has its own special terms. Words such as "folio," "font," and "footer" may mean nothing to the average reader, but to a graphic designer they mean "page number," "typeface," and "text that runs at the bottom of all the pages." Avoid using jargon in your writing.

- Substitute another word for the term you are using.
- If you can't find a substitute, reword your writing to find another way to say what you mean.
- If you have to use the word, make sure you include an explanation or definition of the term.

JUXTAPOSITION

Juxtaposition involves placing two ideas (in words or pictures) together so that their closeness and comparison create a sharp contrast or a new, sometimes ironic meaning. For example, in an advertisement for dandruff shampoo, the image of a person with dandruff on the shoulder could be placed beside a picture of the same person with a dandruff-free shoulder. The advertisement implies that using the shampoo will give the consumer who has dandruff a healthy scalp. Juxtaposition is often used in advertising, but it can be just as effective in narrative.

LEAD

A **lead** is the opening sentence or sentences you write to grab your reader's attention. Different types of leads can be used for different types of writing.

- A lead for a newspaper article is factual, and usually answers the questions *who, what, when, where, why,* and *how*.
- A lead for a story may begin in different ways: with dialogue or with description.
- The lead for an essay begins with an introduction that outlines the main argument.

However you begin your piece, your lead should be interesting and should immediately involve your readers so they'll want to keep reading.

METAPHOR

A **metaphor** is an expression that describes a person, place, or thing by comparing it to something else. A metaphor differs from a simile because it makes a direct comparison without using the words "like" and "as." In the following lines, for example, the colour black is compared to a night sky without any stars.

Black is the night
When there isn't a star
And you can't tell by looking
Where you are.
from "What is Black?" by Mary O'Neill

Metaphors can be useful in many ways.

- They help to create vivid pictures in the readers' minds and spark their imaginations.
- They can help to make abstract ideas concrete (more understandable or real).
- They help to add emotion to a piece of writing or to show the writer's feelings or attitudes about something.
- Metaphors can also say a lot in a small space. A metaphor can say in a few words what it would take a paragraph to explain.
- Sometimes a whole poem could be a metaphor. The comparison is carried throughout the poem.

See **personification** and **simile.**

NARRATION

Narration is the telling in detail of an event or series of events. Narration is used in all types of writing including narrative, personal journals, diaries, plays, and some types of poetry.

See **narrator.**

NARRATOR

The **narrator** is the person or character telling the story. The narrator does not have to be a person, but can be anything you choose. Choosing an interesting narrator can add a special twist to your story. For example, the narrator of *Black Beauty* is a horse that tells the reader her life story.

See **point of view.**

ONOMATOPOEIA

Onomatopoeia is the use of words whose sounds make you think of their meaning. Words such as "buzz," "bang," "hiss," and "screech" sound like the sounds they describe when you say them.

- Onomatopoeia is often used in poetry and advertising to create sounds that are pleasing to the ear.
- Onomatopoeia also adds to the rhythm of the text, and, most important, it reinforces the meaning of the text.

PERSONIFICATION

Personification occurs when the writer describes an animal, an object or thing, or an idea as if it were a person. The stream in the poem below, for example, is described with words usually used in connection to people—"mother" and "bed."

> *Ice mothers me*
> *My bed is rock*
> *Over sand I move silently.*
> from "North Stream" by F.R. Scott

- Personification helps to create vivid pictures in the reader's mind.
- It can also reinforce the meaning of a piece of writing by adding emotion to show how the writer feels about something.
- Personification is most commonly used in poetry, but it can be effective in other types of writing such as narrative, print advertisements, commercials, and jingles.
- Personification is considered a type of metaphor because what is being described is always compared to a person.

See **metaphor**.

WRITING SENSE

PLOT

The **plot** is the action of a story and is made up of a series of events. Every story, whether it is a fantasy, myth, or mystery, has the same elements that can be shown on a plot line. The plot has five parts: the exposition (set-up), rising action, climax, falling action, and resolution.

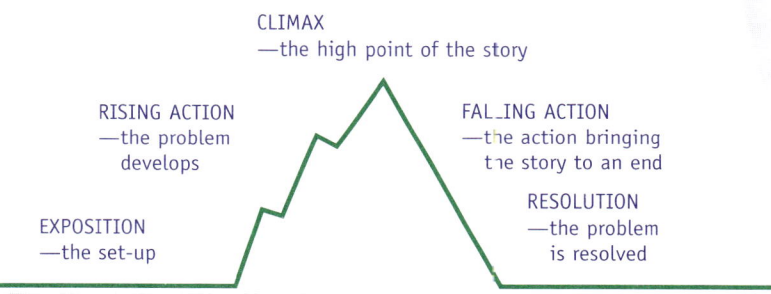

- The exposition sets up the story by introducing the setting and the characters and explaining the background. The exposition is usually the beginning of the story.
- The **rising action** is the main part of a story during which the problem that the protagonist has to solve develops. The rising action involves a number of events that lead up to the climax of the story.
- The **climax** is the highest point in a story where the most exciting, suspenseful, or surprising event occurs. After this point, the problems in the story begin to work out.
- The **falling action** is the part of the story following the climax. It has the action needed to bring the story to an end.
- The **resolution** (sometimes called the dénouement or conclusion) is the end of the story when all the problems are solved.

POINT OF VIEW

The **point of view** is the angle from which the story or information is told and it depends on who is telling the story. There are three main points of view.

- **First person** means the story is told from one character's point of view. In this type of story, all events and conversations are filtered through this person. The pronouns "I," "we," "my," "me," and "mine" are used to show the first person.

  I couldn't believe what happened next. A blast of hot air shot across the room and flattened me against the door.

- **Second person** means the reader is spoken to directly. The author uses the pronouns "you" and "your." The second-person point of view is used mainly in poetry, in create-your-own adventure stories, and in writing where you want to speak directly to your audience, such as in guides or speeches.

  Then you fold the corner of the page into the centre.

- **Third person** means the story is told by an onlooker or narrator. The author uses the pronouns "he," "she," or "they." There are two third-person points of view: omniscient and limited.
  - In the **omniscient** point of view, the narrator knows everything about all of the characters and the events and can shift from character to character showing their thoughts, feelings, and conversations. The narrator can know what is happening in more than one place and at different times.

    One day Jessica decided she'd had enough. It was time to show those MacMullen brothers what she was made of. The MacMullen brothers, however, had other ideas.

  - In the **limited** point of view, the author tells a story from the third person, but describes the actions, thoughts, and feelings of only one character or only a few characters.

- All writing is written from a point of view. Factual writing, such as newspaper articles and research reports, is usually written in the third person, while personal writing, such as diaries and autobiographies, is written in the first person.

See **narrator.**

POINT FORM

Point form is a short form of writing used for taking notes. With point form, you write the main information about different topics in only a few words.

- Include only the main idea.
- Use symbols and abbreviations where possible.
- Include only one idea per point.

PROTAGONIST

The **protagonist** is the main character of a story. The protagonist is important to the story and should be believable to the readers. If a main character is not believable, the readers will not care about what happens to him or her and will not get involved in the story. Protagonists are not necessarily the heroes in a story. Dracula, for example, is a protagonist. The character is believable and interesting, but is not a hero.

- Give your protagonists special characteristics or traits that set them apart from the other characters. They could have unusual talents or even a great sense of humour.
- Make sure your protagonist is believable. Don't create a character that is too "perfect." While your character has to be appealing, too much perfection will be unbelievable.

See **characterization** for ideas about how to describe your characters.

PUN

A **pun** is a word or phrase with more than one possible meaning, used to create a comic effect. Words used in puns are words that sound the same but have different meanings (homophones, homographs) or words that sound nearly the same. Puns are used mainly in jokes and riddles, and sometimes in poetry and scripts.

REPETITION

Repetition is the repeating of a word, phrase, or line to add rhythm or to emphasize an idea. Repetition is used most often in poetry. Robert Louis Stevenson uses repetition to reinforce the meaning in his poem "Windy Nights." Just like the person riding back and forth in the poem, the words have the same motion and are repeated.

> *Whenever the trees are crying aloud,*
> *And ships are tossed at sea,*
> ***By**, on the highway, low and loud,*
> ***By at the gallop** goes he;*
> ***By at the gallop** he goes, and then*
> ***By** he comes back **at the gallop** again.*

- Repetition is also used in advertising—print advertisements, commercials, and jingles—to emphasize the important facts about the product or services being advertised. See **alliteration** for more information about the repetition of sounds within words.

RHYME

Words that **rhyme** sound alike, especially at the ends of the words; for example, "last" and "past," or "clue" and "blue." Many poets use rhyme because it is pleasing to the ear and it gives structure to a poem. Traditional poetry (poetry that follows rules about form and structure, such as a cinquain or sonnet) usually has a lot of rhyme. Rhyme can occur at the end or middle of a line or lines of poetry. End rhyme is the type of rhyme most commonly used by poets, as in the second stanza of Christina Rossetti's poem "Who Has Seen the Wind?"

> *Who has seen the wind?*
> *Neither you nor **I**:*
> *But when the leaves bow down their heads,*
> *The wind is passing **by**.*

- When you want to analyse a rhyming pattern, use the letters a, b, c for the rhyming code and write the appropriate letter at the end of each line. A's rhyme with a's, b's rhyme with b's, and so on. Traditional poetry has many rhyming patterns. Common rhyming patterns are **a a** *b b*; **a** *b* **a** *b*; and **a** *b c b*.

RHYTHM

Rhythm is the occurrence of a beat or a sound in the words of a poem. Think about how you might bob your head or tap your feet to a song you're listening to. You are really tapping out the rhythm. Rhythm is created from the pattern of stressed syllables (those pronounced strongly) and the unstressed syllables (those pronounced weakly) in the words you use. For example:

Twin	kle,	twin	kle,	lit	tle	star
stressed	unstressed	stressed	unstressed	stressed	unstressed	stressed.

All language has a rhythm because all words of more than one syllable have at least one stressed syllable and one or more unstressed syllables.

- Rhythm that has a regular or repeated pattern of stressed and unstressed syllables is called **meter**. Most poetry has a meter, which can be measured in beats or feet.
- A **stanza** is a group of lines whose rhythm pattern or meter is repeated throughout the poem.
- **Free verse** is poetry that does not have a regular meter or rhyme.

SETTING

The **setting** is the time and place where a story happens.

- The setting plays an important role in historical stories where details about the time have to be accurate. Setting is also important in survival stories, adventure stories, science fiction, and fantasy.
- Setting does not play a large role in myths, fables, legends, and pourquoi tales, and is often described in one or two lines.
- When describing the setting, use concrete nouns, verbs, adjectives, and adverbs that bring the scene alive for your reader. Read this description of a setting.

> The hot desert sun beat down in unrelenting waves on Anika's blonde head. Her plane had crashed days ago; she'd only had time to pull herself from the mangled wreckage before it burst into flame. That meant no water, no supplies, no means of transportation.

SIMILE

A **simile** is an expression that describes a person, place, or thing by comparing it to something else. Similes always contain the words "like" or "as" to make the comparison. For example:

He watches from his mountain walls,
*And **like** a thunderbolt he falls.*
from "The Eagle" by Alfred, Lord Tennyson

*An emerald is **as** green **as** grass,*
*A ruby red **as** blood;*
*A sapphire shines **as** blue **as** heaven;*
A flint lies in the mud.
from "Flint" by Christina Rossetti

- Similes are used mainly in poetry and narrative, but are effective in other types of writing such as print advertisements, commercials, or jingles. They help to create vivid pictures in the readers' minds and to create special meaning. In "The Eagle," for example, the poet compares the eagle's ability to move suddenly and quickly to the movement of a thunderbolt. The comparison reveals a lot of information about eagles in only a few words.

See **metaphor**.

SLOGAN

A **slogan** is a short, catchy phrase used in advertising to attract the audience's attention and to sum up the message of the advertisement. Slogans are used on posters, in radio commercials, and in TV commercials. They are usually short, for example, Bell's *Reach Out and Touch Someone,* or Coca-Cola's *Coke Is It* or *Have a Coke and a Smile.*

- A slogan should be easy to remember.
- It should also reflect the character or personality of the product and the tone and atmosphere of the advertisement.

SUSPENSE

Suspense is the feeling of uncertainty or curiosity created by the writer about the outcome of a story, novel, or play, or any kind of poetry that tells a story. Suspense is important to all types of stories because as a writer you want your reader to keep reading on to find out what is going to happen, when, and to whom.

- Suspense is especially effective in mysteries, survival stories, and adventure stories because it helps to create the feeling of danger and excitement that is so important to these formats.
- You can create suspense through the events and conflicts you include in your story.

See **cliff-hanger** and **foreshadowing.**

SYMBOL

A **symbol** is a person, place, thing, or event that is used to represent something else. For example, a dove is often used as a symbol of peace. Symbols should be used sparingly in your writing. There is a chance that your reader will not know what the symbol means.

- If you use a symbol, make sure its meaning is clear to your reader.
- Commonly used symbols include a rainbow as the sign of hope, and a white flag as a symbol of surrender.

THEME

A **theme** is the main idea or message in a story or novel. By selecting a theme, the writer is sharing a belief or idea about life with the reader. For example, in *Anne of Green Gables*, the theme is accepting people for who they are. By the end of the story, Anne's adoptive family comes to accept her uniqueness.

- Before you begin writing a story, you might think about what, if anything, you would like your story to tell your reader. You may just want to entertain your reader with an exciting story, or you may wish to share an idea that you feel is important.

TONE

The **tone** is the expression of the author's feeling or attitude about the subject. The tone in a piece of writing may be serious, sad, funny, angry, and so on. For example, in a speech about pollution, the author may be angry about how much pollution there is, and use emotional language to show this feeling.

- Keep in mind that different types of writing should have different tones. A friendly letter, for example, should be casual and friendly because you know the person you are writing to, and it is written in the first-person point of view. A persuasive essay should have an objective and formal tone (factual, with no personal opinions). You can accomplish this by using the third-person point of view.

See **point of view.**

VOICE

Voice is how a writer expresses his or her ideas and information in a piece of writing. Voice involves the tone (the writer's feelings about the subject) and the writer's style (how ideas and information are put together in sentences and paragraphs). Everyone has a voice of his or her own that is unique to that person. To develop your own voice

- write about topics that interest you
- remember that the tone you choose is affected by your purpose for writing and your audience
- work on your writing style
    - Practise often. Keep a diary or journal, and write in it every day. Try different techniques such as metaphors, personification, and onomatopoeia.
    - Write with details. Use these details to help your readers feel as if they are right there with you.
    - Write in different formats. Try an article, a story, or a poem.
    - Look at what other writers have written. Examine the way they put sentences and paragraphs together.

See **tone.**

TOOL KIT

The Tool Kit is a reference section you can refer to as you plan, draft, revise, and edit your writing. It's organized into five sections—Conducting Research, Grammar and Usage, Punctuation, Spelling, and Word Power—to help you find the specific information you need. See the section contents listed below.

Conducting Research 154
- Taking Notes
- Using the Library
- Other Sources

Grammar and Usage 160
- Parts of Speech
- Parts of a Sentence
- Sentences
- Common Sentence Problems
- Paragraphs

Punctuation 175
- Apostrophes
- Capitalization
- Colons
- Commas
- Dashes
- Ellipses
- Exclamation Marks
- Parentheses and Brackets
- Periods
- Question Marks
- Quotation Marks
- Semicolons
- Slashes

Spelling 181
- Abbreviations
- Alternate Spellings
- Commonly Misspelled Words
- Contractions
- Homophones and Homographs
- Numbers
- Spelling Strategies

Word Power 187
- Antonyms
- Appropriate Language
- Commonly Misused Words
- Synonyms
- Using Dictionaries
- Using Thesauruses

Evaluating Sources

It's important to evaluate the sources in any research you conduct. Just because information is printed does not necessarily mean it's true or that it gives the "whole story." Check that the source is up to date and that the author is respected.

Keep in mind that books that are published by organizations that might have sponsored the book could show bias in their information.

Compare the information in a variety of sources to see how they handled the subject and to check for accuracy.

Conducting Research

You will need to conduct research for some formats of writing; for example, for newspaper and magazine articles, and speeches. There are steps you can follow that will help make your researching easier.

1. Focus on your topic. Jot down what you already know about it, and make a list of questions about the topic you want to have answered.
2. Think about where you might find the information you need. There are many sources of information. (See Using the Library, pages 156–159.)
3. Learn how to find your information easily and quickly. Knowing how to use indexes, catalogues, and computer technology is helpful. If you don't know how to use any of these items, ask a teacher, school librarian, or your classmates for help.

Taking Notes

The research notes you take are very important because the information and facts you use will come from these notes. When taking notes, make sure you do the following.

- Record the title and author of the source, and the place and date it was published. You can use index cards, with one source on each card. This will come in handy when you use direct quotations, or write a bibliography or reference list.
- Write down the page numbers of the information you find. You might need to refer back to the pages to check for additional information.
- Include only the main information and put it in your own words. This will avoid the problem of mistakenly copying someone else's words. (This is called plagiarism and it is illegal.)
- Use your own short forms, abbreviations, contractions, and symbols to help you write quickly. Make sure any shortcuts in writing you use are clear and make sense.

Bibliography (Reference List)

Some types of writing, such as research reports or persuasive essays, should include a bibliography or reference list.

- Arrange the list in alphabetical order by author.
- For sources with no author, use the name of the book.
- Remember that "a," "an," and "the" do not count. Check out the examples listed below for organization, style, and punctuation.

Books
- One author
Author (last name first). Title (in italics). City where the book is published: Publisher, copyright date.
Karmen, Steve. *Through the Jingle Jungle: The Art and Business of Making Music for Commercials*. New York: Billboard Books, 1989.
- Two or three authors
Lottridge, Celia Barker, and Alison Dickie. *Mythic Voices: Reflections in Mythology*. Toronto: Nelson Canada, 1991.

Magazine and Newspaper Articles
Author (last name first). "Title of article" (in quotation marks). Title of magazine or newspaper (in italics), Date (day/month/year): Page numbers of the article.
Todd, Dave. "Keeping the Peace." *Canadian Geographic*, Nov./Dec. 1992: 56-64.
Meikle, Marg. "Getting Connected." *The Toronto Star*, 9 June 1996: E6.

Encyclopedias
"Article title" (in quotation marks). Title of the reference book (italics). Edition. Date published.
"Whale Oil." *The New Encyclopaedia Britannica*. 15th ed. 1985.

Slides, Videotapes, Films
Title (italics). Medium (videocassette, film, slides). Production company, date.
The Global Citizen from Scanning Television: Videos for Media Literacy in Class. Videotape. Face to Face Media and the Jesuit Communication Project, 1996.

CD-ROM
Author (if known). Title (italics). Publisher, year. Type of software.
Rivers of Canada. Harcourt Brace & Company, Canada, Ltd., Canadian Geographic Enterprises, and Medium Cool, 1997. CD-ROM.

Using the Library

The library is usually the best place to start your research. You can find a wide variety of print and non-print sources at most libraries. Remember to keep a list of the sources you use.

Vertical Files

For current information, most libraries keep filing cabinets with files containing magazine and newspaper clippings and pamphlets on many subjects. These are called *vertical files*. They are usually arranged in alphabetical order by subject.

Non-Fiction Books

Non-fiction books in the library contain a wealth of information. To find specific information quickly and easily, use the organizational tools of the book.

The **preface**, **foreword**, or **introduction** comes immediately before or after the table of contents. They tell you what the book is about and why it was written.

The **table of contents** lists what is in the book and which page to find it on. The contents are usually arranged by chapter or subject headings.

An **appendix** follows the main sections of the book. Appendices contain extra information such as charts, tables, diagrams, maps, letters, or copies of official documents, and are referenced throughout the book.

A **glossary** gives the meaning of unusual or special words that may have been used in the book. The glossary is usually at the back of the book.

A **bibliography** lists other books or articles published on a particular topic. It could be a list of information sources used in writing the book or it may be a list of books by a certain author. You can use the list to find other books on the same topic.

An **index** lists key words, main topics, and names found in the book in alphabetical order and gives page numbers so you can easily find the information.

Print Sources

You will probably be familiar with encyclopedias, but there are some other print sources that you may not be familiar with. These include almanacs, yearbooks, periodicals (magazines, journals, newspapers), biographical dictionaries, books of quotations, directories, and atlases. Ask your librarian where to find these.

- An **encyclopedia** is a book or books full of information about a variety of subjects. They have articles, definitions, photographs, and diagrams of things, events, places, and people. Today most encyclopedias can be found on CD-ROMs. There are also specialized encyclopedias on only one subject.
- **Almanacs** are yearly calendars that contain statistics of various kinds.
- **Yearbooks** may contain a chronicle of the events that took place in a given year. The information is arranged by subject. Some yearbooks may focus on one subject area; for example, the arts or politics.
- **Periodicals** contain articles on a wide variety of subjects. To make it easier to find articles, most libraries have indexes of magazine and journal articles, such as *The Reader's Guide to Periodical Literature*.
- **Biographical Dictionaries** are a useful source of information about people. They offer biographies of artists, authors, musicians, scientists, politicians, and other well-known people. *Canadian Who's Who*, for example, gives short biographies of well-known people in Canada.
- **Books of quotations** contain interesting often-quoted words of famous people and writers. Check out *Bartlett's Familiar Quotations* or *The Oxford Dictionary of Quotations*.
- **Directories** are a good place to find out the names of companies and organizations where you may find further information.
- An **atlas** contains maps. Check out the *Historical Atlas of Canada* or the *Oxford Canadian Atlas of the World*.

Computer Sources

You can use online computer searches and CD-ROMs to conduct research.

- **CD-ROMs** can hold books, pictures, indexes, encyclopedias, and much more. Remember that you cannot add to or change the information on the CD-ROM. You can often borrow CD-ROMs from the library and most bookstores offer a wide variety.

- **Online data bases** can also be useful. There are many data bases (files of information) that you can tap into. They range from encyclopedias, news summaries, and newspaper articles to magazine articles and biographical profiles. All you need is a computer, a telephone line, and a modem (a device that lets computer data be transmitted by phone).
- The **World Wide Web** (the Web for short) is becoming the most popular feature of the Internet. The Web uses electronic pages that display text and pictures similar to the pages in a book. It can also play sound and video. To get to a specific Web site, all you need is the address. Key it in and you'll go right to that site. Once you're there, just click on the graphics or click on the underlined or highlighted words with your mouse.

Audio-Visual Sources

Videos are produced on a variety of topics and on specific subject areas, such as science, history, or the arts. You can borrow them from your local library or video store and screen them at home or school. Some libraries may also have VCRs you can use.

Libraries may also have compact disks, cassettes, multimedia kits, and films. Ask your librarian for more information.

Other Sources

E-mail

Try e-mailing someone in your community (your local MP, for example) to find information. E-mail (electronic mail) is the fastest way to send a letter anywhere in the world. All you need is the e-mail address of the person you're sending a message to and access to the Internet.

When you are typing an e-mail address, type every character into your computer exactly as you see it. Don't leave any spaces, and double-check the address before you send your message.

- The **to** line is the address of the person receiving the message.
- The **from** line contains the address of the person sending the message.
- The **subject** line tells what the message is about in a few words.
- The **message** is the letter part of the e-mail.
- **Attachments** are any text files that you add to your e-mail message.

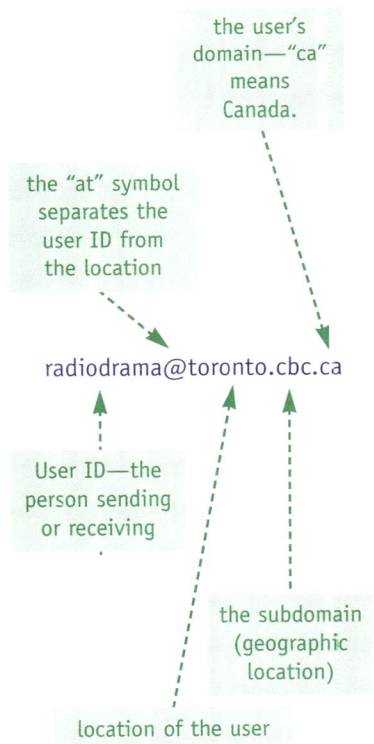

Interviews

An interview with an expert can be one of the best ways to get accurate, up-to-date information. Here are a few helpful ideas for conducting an interview.

1. Decide who you want to interview and why.
2. Research your topic and develop a list of questions. Ask open-ended questions that will give you a lot of information; for example: *Tell me about yourself.* Avoid questions that can be answered yes or no.
3. Make an appointment, and arrange a time and place for the interview. Explain what you want to talk about and ask if you can use a tape recorder.
4. Ask a friend to check your questions, and practise reading them.
5. During the interview
   - introduce yourself and remind your subject of the purpose of the interview
   - look and act interested, and make eye contact
   - take careful notes (even if you are taping the interview, make notes in case something goes wrong with your tape recorder)
   - ask follow-up questions (questions that come to mind as your guest talks)
   - if you don't understand something, ask for an explanation
6. After the interview, thank your guest, check the spelling of any names, and organize your notes as soon as you can.

Surveys

Surveys are another good way to get information and are best for finding out what people think about a particular subject. Here are a few helpful ideas for conducting a survey.

1. Decide exactly what you want to know, and make a list of questions.
2. Decide whom you'll survey—other students, your teachers, or people in your community. Whom you survey depends on what you are trying to find out.
3. Include a section in the survey for the age, gender, and occupation of the people you survey.
4. Develop a questionnaire (a typed list of questions that can be filled in) to hand out to gather your data.
5. Organize your results. What did you find? What conclusions did you come to? Will you use charts or will you graph the results to show trends?

Grammar and Usage

Grammar is the set of rules that determines how words are put together in certain patterns. **Usage** is the way these grammatical patterns are used to form sentences and paragraphs.

This section explains the eight different parts of speech and the parts of a sentence, and what they do. It also describes types of sentences and paragraphs and gives suggestions for solving common sentence problems.

Parts of Speech

Parts of speech are the names for words grouped according to how they are used in a sentence. If you understand the role that each part of speech plays in a sentence and the rules it follows, you can put sentences together correctly and effectively.

Nouns

A **noun** is a person (*Jason, mother*), place (*home, Edmonton*), thing (*book, coat*), or idea (*peace, democracy*). There are many kinds of nouns.

- **Common nouns** are the names of any member of a group (*a nurse, the house, the tree, a hope*). These nouns are *not* the specific names of things or people.
- **Proper nouns** are the names of specific people, places, things, or ideas (*Aunt Eva, Buddhism*). These nouns usually start with a capital letter.
- **Possessive nouns** show that something belongs to a person, place, thing, or idea. Possessive nouns are made by adding 's to singular nouns (*Sandy's hat*) or by adding an apostrophe only to plural nouns (*babies' bottles*).
- **Compound nouns** are usually made up of two or more nouns that express one idea (*doghouse, brother-in-law, tennis match*).
- **Concrete nouns** name things that can be seen or touched (*computers, Lake Ontario*). **Abstract nouns** name ideas and feelings (*friendship, love*).

> **TIP**
>
> If the noun you are using as the subject is plural, make sure the verb you use is also plural.
>
> *Eleni runs.*
> *Diego and Tim run.*

Pronouns

Pronouns are used like nouns and can take the place of a noun. In the sentence, *Sheena said **she** didn't know*, *she* takes the place of *Sheena*.

- Some pronouns take the place of a person or persons, or a thing. A pronoun agrees with the noun it replaces in number (*singular* or *plural*) and gender (*masculine* or *feminine*).
- Some pronouns refer to specific people or things (*I, you, he, she, it, we, they, me, him, her, us, them, mine, yours, his, hers, its, ours, theirs*).
  *After Kiko read **my** book, **he** gave **it** back to **me**.*
  (*He* refers to Kiko, *it* refers to the book, and *my* and *me* refer to the speaker.)
- Some pronouns refer to general or unspecified persons or things (*all, any, anybody, anything, both, each, either, everyone, few, many, no one, none, other, several, some, something*). Others refer to specific people, places, things, or ideas (*that, these, this, those*). They are used to point out things nearby or far away.
  *Has **anybody** read this book?   **Those** are my shoes.*
- Some pronouns take the place of a noun that comes earlier in a sentence or they begin phrases (*that, which, who, whom, whose*) and others introduce questions (*what, which, who, whom, whose*).
  *I gave the book to Diane **who** gave it to Chris.   **What** was that noise?*

Verbs

Verbs are words that show action or a state of being. Verbs show what the subject does or has done to it.

- An **action verb** tells what the subject of the sentence is doing.
  *I **played** tennis yesterday.   Naomi **left** me a message to call her back.*
- A **linking verb** shows a state of being.
  *The water **look**s black in the moonlight.*
- A **helping verb** comes before the main verb and helps it to do its job.
  *I **will** go to the movies tomorrow.   Tamara **may** visit me in the summer.*
  Other helping verbs include *be, being, been, am, are, is, was, were, shall, could, would, should, might, just, can, have, had, has, do,* and *did*.

Singular and Plural

- **Verbs** show how many people are doing the action. If only one person or thing does the action, then the verb is in the *singular*. If there is more than one, then the verb is in the *plural*.

SINGULAR	PLURAL
She sings	*They sing*
I am	*We are*

Tense

- The **tense** of a verb shows when the action happens—in the past, the present (now), or the future.

PAST TENSE	*I walked the dog.*	*I was walking the dog.*
	I have walked the dog.	*I had walked the dog.*
PRESENT TENSE	*I walk the dog.*	*I am walking the dog.*
FUTURE TENSE	*I will walk the dog.*	

Active and Passive Voice

Voice shows whether the subject is acting or being acted upon.
- Verbs can be in the **active voice** or the **passive voice.**
  - Active voice means the subject of the verb is acting or doing something.
    *I **hit** the ball.*   *I **served** dinner.*
  - Passive voice means the action is happening to the subject.
    *Chanda **was hit** by the ball.*   *Dinner **was served**.*
- The passive voice is made by adding different forms of the verb *to be* to the verb.
  *The truck **was hit**.*   *The dishes **were washed**.*

> **TIP**
> Avoid using the passive voice in your writing. The active voice is clearer and more direct and it adds more life to your writing than the passive voice.

Adjectives

Adjectives are words that describe, limit, or identify a noun or pronoun. They tell the quality, quantity, or order of a noun. The word used to describe what adjectives do is *modify*. There are many kinds of adjectives.
- **Descriptive adjectives** add details and answer the questions *What is it like?* and *What kind?*
  *The **white** owl hooted and flew into the night.*

162   WRITING SENSE

- **Limiting adjectives** make nouns and pronouns more specific and answer the questions *Which one? How many?* and *How much?*
  *I read **two** books on the weekend.*
- Most adjectives come before the noun they are describing.
  *The **grey** mouse*
  Others come after the verb *to be* and linking verbs such as *to become, to see,* and *to appear.*
  *The door was **open**.*   *She seems **happy**.*
- Sometimes two or more adjectives describe the same noun.
  – If the adjectives are equally important, separate them with a comma.
     *A **happy, confident** team* (The team is both happy and confident.)
  – If the first adjective modifies the second adjective, do not add a comma.
     *A **dark blue** sea* (The sea is a dark blue colour.)

> **TIP**
> Use adjectives that are as specific as possible. Instead of writing a *good* coat, you could write a *warm* coat or a *waterproof* coat.

Adverbs

Adverbs are words that describe a verb, adjective, or adverb. The word used to describe what adverbs do is *modify*.
*Asad ate **quickly**.* (*Quickly* modifies the verb *ate*.)
*Carol made a **carefully** drawn map.* (*Carefully* modifies the adjective *drawn*.)
*Juanita walked **very** slowly.* (*Very* modifies the adverb *slowly*.)

- Adverbs explain the action of a verb in terms of **where** (in what place), **how** (in what manner), **degree** (how much), **when** (at what time), or **how often** something happens.

where	Sit **here**.	**when**	I'll leave **soon**.
how	Look **carefully**!	**how often**	She **always** eats here.
degree	It's too **hot**!		

- Adverbs are usually put as close as possible to the word they modify.
- Some adverbs modify the whole sentence. Where these adverbs are placed affects the emphasis of the sentence.
  ***Quickly**, I rushed home to finish my homework.*
  *I rushed home to **quickly** finish my homework.*
  *I rushed home to finish my homework **quickly**.*

> **TIP**
> Some adverbs have two forms (*cheap/cheaply, loud/loudly, direct/directly, quick/quickly, slow/slowly, sure/surely, wide/widely*). The shorter form is usually considered less formal but stronger.

TOOL KIT

Comparative Forms of Adjectives and Adverbs

Most adjectives and adverbs can show how much of a quality the word being modified has. This chart shows how to spell the different forms.

	REGULAR	COMPARATIVE	SUPERLATIVE
Add *er* and *est* to the REGULAR FORM:	high	higher	highest
	quick	quicker	quickest
	hungry	hungrier	hungriest
Add *more* or *most*:	helpful	more helpful	most helpful
Add *less* or *least*:	easily	less easily	least easily
IRREGULAR:	good or well	better	best
	bad	worse	worst
	far	farther	farthest

Conjunctions

Conjunctions are words or phrases that connect words, phrases, clauses, or sentences.

- Conjunctions that join nouns with nouns, verbs with verbs, clauses with clauses, or sentences with sentences, and so on, are *and, but, for, or, not, so,* and *yet.* A comma usually goes before the conjunctions that join clauses or sentences.
  You can have an apple, an orange, **or** a banana.
  I read a book, **but** Sunni watched TV.

- Some conjunctions join dependent clauses. These conjunctions include *after, although, as, because, before, even though, if, however, in order to, now that, rather than, since, that, unless, until, when, where, whether,* and *while.*
  Now that the babysitter is here, I can leave.
  I stayed **until** the game was over.

TIP

If you write a lot of short sentences, try joining some of them with conjunctions. This will make your writing smoother and more interesting to read.

Prepositions

A **preposition** shows when, where, how, and why things happen. Prepositions are not used on their own—they need a noun or a pronoun to finish the thought.
- Prepositions show
  - **when** something happens (*after, before, during, since,* and *until*)
  We had hot chocolate **after** the game.
  - **where** something takes place (*above, across, along, among, at, behind, between, by, from, in, near, on, out,* and *up*)
  Greg sat **between** Tara and Jenny.
  - **how** something is done (*by means of, for, in spite of, like,* and *with*)
  Don't bike **without** a helmet.
  - **why** something happens (*for, to,* and *at*)
  He jumped **for** joy.

Interjections

An **interjection** is a short word, phrase, or sentence that breaks the flow of a thought.
- Some interjections express a feeling or emotion.
  Wow! No way! Get out!
- Some interjections are sound words.
  Psst. Hmmm. Hey!
- Interjections are followed by an exclamation point if the emotion is strong.
  Help! I can't open the door.

If the emotion is not strong, use a comma or dash.
Well, what do you think?

- Most interjections stand alone, but if they come in the middle of a sentence, they should be surrounded with commas or dashes.
  We're going to climb the mountain, and—**I hope**—we're going to make it.

TIP

Many people still think it is wrong to end a sentence with a preposition, but it is correct to do so. Make your own decision about where to place the preposition by the way the sentence sounds. For example:

*Where did this book come **from?***

sounds better than

***From** where did this book come?*

Or

*What are you looking **at?***

sounds better than

***At** what are you looking?*

TIP

Be careful not to overuse interjections. Save them to show genuine emotion.

Parts of a Sentence

All the parts of a sentence work together to express a complete thought. Every sentence has a **subject** and a **predicate**. Together the subject and predicate are a complete thought and can stand alone.

Subject

The **subject** is the person, place, thing, or idea being discussed in the sentence (it's what the sentence is about). The subject is usually a noun or a pronoun.
Kyoko danced the tango.   The **big, red car** stopped suddenly.

Predicate

The **predicate** is the part of the sentence that explains what the subject is doing or what is said about the subject. The predicate can be one word or many words, but it always has a verb.
Tony **laughed**.   The big, red car **sped off into the night.**

Object

Sometimes the predicate contains an **object.** An object receives the action of the verb.
- A **direct object** answers the question *what* or *who*. In the following sentence, *Hanif's bike* is the direct object.
  Tonya borrowed **Hanif's bike.**
- An **indirect object** answers the questions *to whom, for whom, to what,* or *for what* something is done. In the following sentence, *me* is the indirect object.
  Tonya lent **me** Hanif's bike.

Phrases

A **phrase** is a group of words that expresses an idea, but it doesn't make a sentence on its own. There are different kinds of phrases.
Walking up a hill is good exercise. (a noun phrase)
Katie will have left by now. (a verb phrase)
The house **beside my aunt's house** is for sale. (an adjective phrase)
He chased the dog **around the park**. (an adverb phrase)

Clauses

A **clause** is a group of words that has a **subject** (a noun) and a **predicate** (a verb, and sometimes adjectives, adverbs, and phrases).
- An **independent** or **main clause** is a complete thought. It can stand alone (it doesn't need anything else to make it a sentence).
  I saw a movie last night.   I enjoyed it.
- A **dependent** or **subordinate clause** is not a complete thought and doesn't make sense by itself. Dependent clauses are always used with a main clause to make a complete sentence.
  Although the movie was long, *I enjoyed it.*
  *I like to go out **whenever I get the chance.***

Words that introduce dependent clauses include *after, although, as, because, before, if, once, since, that, unless, until, what, when, where, while, who,* and *whose.*

> **TIP**
> You can add interest to your writing by changing where you put the dependent clauses—at the beginning of the sentence, at the end, or in the middle.

Sentences

A **sentence** expresses a complete thought. It has a subject and a predicate, and it begins with a capital letter and ends with a period, question mark, or exclamation mark.

- Sentences express information in four ways.
  STATEMENT: *This is my pen.*
  COMMAND: *Hold my pen.*
  QUESTION: *Where's my pen?*
  EXCLAMATION: *That's my pen!*
- Sentences are structured (formed) in three ways.
  – A **simple sentence** has one main clause.
    I like fishing.
  – A **compound sentence** has two or more main clauses. (They are joined by conjunctions such as *but, and, for, or, so,* and *yet.*)
    I like fishing, but I don't like camping.
  – A **complex sentence** has one or more dependent clauses.
    Because I like fishing, I learned to make lures.

> **TIP**
> The length and style of your sentences depend on what you are writing. For example, instructions are often clearer written in short, simple sentences; descriptive passages can be more effective in longer, complex sentences.

Transitional Expressions

Transitional expressions provide links between your thoughts; for example, *I'm going to the library,* **then** *to dinner.* They explain how and why you are connecting ideas and help your reader to follow your pattern of thought. You may need to use any of the following transitional expressions within sentences, between sentences, or even between paragraphs to make it easy for your reader to understand what you are saying.

To compare or add a point

again	another	furthermore	like
also	in addition	next	and
as well (as)	just	or	and yet
by comparison	as	the same as	too

To summarize or conclude

as a result	to summarize	finally	to sum up
that is	in summary	in conclusion	then
therefore	in other words	in brief	to repeat

To add emphasis

above all	in fact	most of all	certainly
in particular	particularly	especially	more important

To show a sequence

again	at last	last	to begin with
also	finally	moreover	too
and	further	next	(first, second, third)
and then	in addition	still	(in the first place, in the second place)

To express cause and effect

and so	otherwise	as a result	for that reason
then	since	consequently	therefore

To show time

after a while	afterward	as soon as	soon
until	at the same time	at this time	before
earlier	eventually	finally	immediately
until now	lately	now	in the meantime
when	later	meanwhile	next

To show location

above	across	at	far
behind	below	beside	in front of
beyond	distant	to	as near as
here	near	on the right	toward
on	on the left	under	opposite

Common Sentence Problems

Run-On Sentences

Run-on sentences are a common sentence problem. A run-on sentence occurs when two or more sentences are joined together by only a comma or written as one sentence with no punctuation.
- When you are revising your writing and you notice a sentence with more than one idea that doesn't make sense, it is probably a run-on sentence.
  I saw a movie Saturday it was about tornadoes.
  I saw a movie Saturday, it was about tornadoes.
- Use these suggestions to fix run-on sentences.
  - Use a period to make separate sentences.
    I saw a movie Saturday night. It was about tornadoes.
  - Connect the sentences with a comma and a conjunction such as *and, but, so, for, or, nor,* or *yet.*
    I saw a movie Saturday night, **and** *it was about tornadoes.*
  - Connect the sentences with a semicolon.
    I saw a movie Saturday night; it was about tornadoes.

Sentence Fragments

A **sentence fragment** is an incomplete thought. It may have a capital letter and punctuation, but it is not a sentence. For it to be a sentence, the thought needs to be completed.
FRAGMENT: *When I go on vacation.*
COMPLETE: *When I go on vacation, I ask my sister to take care of my pets.*
- Use these suggestions to help you revise sentence fragments.
  - Try attaching the fragment to the sentence that comes before or after it.
    FRAGMENT: *Kim likes to read. Mainly mystery stories.*
    COMPLETE: *Kim likes to read mainly mystery stories.*
  - Turn the fragment into a complete sentence.
    Kim reads mainly mystery stories.

Sentence Agreement

Make sure that the parts of your sentences agree with one another. If you use a singular subject, the verb should be singular as well. If you use a plural subject, the verb should be plural too. Check out the examples below.

- **One subject**
  Sanjih likes *the book I gave him for his birthday.*
  (*Sanjih* and *likes* agree because they are both singular.)
  My **brothers went** *to the movies.*
  (*Brothers* and *went* agree because they are both plural.)
- **Compound subjects**
  – Compound subjects connected by *and* need a plural verb.
  Carla and Ravi are *good swimmers.*
  – In sentences with compound subjects connected by *or*, the verb should agree with the subject nearest to it.
  Either Jane or **Paul needs** *to meet you at the airport.*
  (A singular verb is needed because *Paul* is singular.)
  Janet or her **parents have** *to sign the contract.*
  (A plural verb is needed because *parents* is plural.)

Sentence Variety

Make your writing more interesting by arranging the words in your sentences in different ways or by using different types of sentences and sentence structure.

- **Combine your sentences.** Turn short, choppy sentences into longer, more flowing ones.
  SEPARATE: *The wood was damp. It burned slowly.*
  COMBINED: *The damp wood burned slowly.*
- **Invert your sentences.** Change the natural order of the words in sentences. If too many of your sentences begin the same way, your writing will be dull.
  – Begin with what happened and follow with the subject.
  NATURAL: *The deer raced through the forest.*
  INVERTED: *Through the forest raced the deer.*
  – Start with an adjective or adverb. **Quietly,** *she tiptoed across the dark room.*
  – Begin with a phrase. **Excited by the noise,** *the baby bounced up and down.*
  – Start with a clause. **The dragon roared,** *and I became afraid.*

- **Use different sentence types.** Use questions, exclamations, statements, or commands.
- **Use a variety of sentence structures.** A mix of simple, compound, and complex sentences will help you to add details and information.

Paragraphs

A **paragraph** is one or more related sentences about one main idea.

- A paragraph should have a topic sentence that states the main idea. The other sentences support or develop this main idea, and are closely related to it.
- Start a new paragraph every time a new person speaks or when a new idea, location, time, or person enters the writing. The first line of each new paragraph is indented. Sometimes a blank line separates paragraphs.

topic sentence

body (supporting details)

Swimming, while a fun activity, can be dangerous if you aren't careful, so follow these simple, commonsense rules to make sure you have a safe dip. First, never go swimming alone. Always swim with a friend in case something goes wrong. Your friend can help you out or go to get help. Second, never swim in a place you're not familiar with. If you know the area you're swimming in, it's less likely that you'll get into trouble. Third, never swim out too far. If you get a cramp, it will be much easier to get back to shore. Lastly, know your own limitations and don't push yourself. If you follow these simple rules, a safe swim is guaranteed.

closing sentence

Organizing a Paragraph

There are different ways you can organize a paragraph around your main idea or topic sentence.

- Begin your paragraph with a broad topic sentence, then add supporting details that slowly narrow down to a focus on the main idea at the end of the paragraph.
- Place your topic sentence at the end of the paragraph. You can then develop the paragraph from the bottom up by adding the details.
- Begin your paragraph with a topic sentence and end by restating it. The supporting details should come between the two.
- You can also put the topic sentence in the middle of the paragraph. Build up to the topic sentence by adding details that increase in importance. After the topic sentence, continue the paragraph to a closing sentence that provides a transition to the next paragraph.

Types of Paragraphs

There are different types of paragraphs for different types of writing. For example, a dialogue paragraph is used mainly in narrative; a persuasive paragraph is used to convince readers. There are five main types of paragraphs you can use in your writing.

- A **descriptive** paragraph describes a person, place, thing, or idea. It makes your reader see, hear, smell, taste, and feel what you are describing.
  - Use specific nouns, verbs, adjectives, and adverbs to create the description of the person, place, or thing.
  - Add details so that the reader can picture exactly what you're describing. Appeal to the five senses.
  - Use writing techniques such as metaphors, similes, and personification.

> The baby dragon's skin was as bright red as a shiny apple. His huge, blue eyes made a startling contrast against his red skin. He kept trying to get to his feet, but at each wobbly attempt his newborn legs gave out, and with a plop, he fell down. With a humanlike snort and a look of determination, he flapped his thin, tiny wings, and picked himself up for another try.

- A **narrative** paragraph tells a story by sharing the details of an event or experience. It's important to include a lot of detail to make the event or experience come alive for your reader. Use this type of paragraph in narrative and other types of writing when you want to tell a story.
  - Set the scene with your opening paragraph.
  - Choose a point of view to write from—first person, second person, or third person.

> As I approached the inner courtyard, I saw a puff of smoke rising above the wall. It was accompanied by the loudest bellow I'd ever heard. Not far behind the sound, barrelled Kermit. At three months old, he was big. In fact he was much bigger than the last time I saw him. Loaded down with my pack I couldn't get out of the way of the whirlwind approaching me. It was almost comical watching him trying to slow down. But it was too late. With a bone-jarring crash, Kermit smashed into me.

- A **persuasive** paragraph expresses the writer's opinion about a topic or subject and tries to convince the reader to agree with it. An argument is made with supporting details and examples to prove the writer's point of view.
  - State your main argument.
  - Include supporting details to prove it.

> If you think that by recycling you're doing enough for the environment, think again. Ask yourself the following questions: What is the quality of the air I breathe every day? Can I go swimming at the nearest beach? What is the condition of the ozone? Do I hear daily warnings about ultraviolet rays on the radio? If you've answered in the negative to any of these questions, you need to take action to ensure a healthy, clean world for future generations.

> **TIP**
>
> Use these questions to help you develop and revise your paragraphs.
> - Have I used the right type of paragraph for my purpose?
> - Is the main idea clear? Is it fully developed?
> - Do I have enough details, reasons, and examples to support the main idea?
> - Is all the information relevant to the main idea?
> - Does the information flow from sentence to sentence?

- An **instructional** or **expository** paragraph gives step-by-step instructions about how to do something. It may explain ideas and give directions as well. It uses transitional expressions, such as "first," "second," and "then," to show a sequence or order.
  - State your topic sentence or main idea.
  - Organize your instructions in a logical order. You can use words such as "first," "second," and so on.

> Making a whirl-i-gig is very easy to do. First, lay a two-litre plastic bottle on its side and trace three 8 cm x 3 cm rectangles equal distances apart along the curved surface of the bottle. Second, use a utility knife to cut along three sides of each rectangle. Pull the cut edges of the rectangle out, and fold the cut pieces along the uncut side of the rectangle. Then put a 2 cm x 1 m dowel into the spout end of the bottle until it touches the bottom of the bottle. Lastly, stick the whirl-i-gig into the ground in an open area where it can catch a lot of wind. Then watch it whirl!

- An **explanatory** paragraph explains an experience, event, or circumstance, and often answers the questions *who, what, when, where, why,* and *how*. It may use description, comparison and contrast, and sometimes cause-and-effect relationships to make the explanation clear.
  - State your topic sentence.
  - Support the topic sentence with detailed information.

> Nobody knows for sure why the population of Mohenjo-Daro died out. Using soil samples, we determined that a severe flood caused by an earthquake did a great deal of damage to the buildings and that the city suffered periodic flooding. There is also evidence of a military invasion.

WRITING SENSE

Punctuation

Punctuation helps the reader to read a group of words as if they were spoken. For example, periods and commas show when there is a pause between words. Following the rules of punctuation makes it easier for a reader to read and understand what you have written.

Apostrophes

Apostrophes (') have two uses in written English.
- In contractions, they show that some letters or numbers are missing.
  she's (she is), *won't* (will not), *o'clock* (of the clock), *'99* (1999)
- They show possession or ownership.
  Lekh's idea, Sunjay's dinner, the boy's clothes
  - For singular nouns that end in **s**, you can use ' or 's.
    Luis' dog or *Luis's dog   my boss' desk* or *my boss's desk*
  - For plural nouns that end in **s**, you only add the apostrophe.
    the girls' clubhouse   the babies' jackets

Capitalization

Capital letters are used in the following places.
- The first word of any sentence.
  Where are we going now?
- People's names and other proper nouns.
  Dennis Lee, the Calgary Stampede, Canada Day
- The pronoun "I."
  I can't believe what I just did.
- The first word of a direct quotation.
  Sarah asked, "Where did you leave the keys?"

TIP

When a compound noun using a proper name becomes common as in *melba toast*, *french fries*, *kraft paper*, and *bunsen burner*, the capital letter is dropped.

Colons

A **colon** (:) tells the reader to "note what follows." Colons are used

- to introduce a list of items. Often, a word or phrase such as *these*, *for example*, or *the following* comes before the colon.
  You'll need to bring the following items: a bathing suit, a towel, and sunscreen.
- at the beginning of an explanation of what has just been said.
  My vacation was horrible: my luggage was lost, and it rained all the time.
- after the greeting in a formal letter.
  Dear Ms. Manley: *Dear Dr. Lopez:*
- when writing the time in numbers.
  4:15   *6:30*
- to introduce a quotation that is four or more lines long.
- in a script, to separate the characters' names from the spoken words or dialogue.

Commas

A **comma** (,) makes writing easier to read and understand. Commas generally show where a natural pause occurs in a sentence. They never go between the subject and verb. Commas are placed

- before a conjunction (*and*, *but*, *or*) joining main clauses.
  The sun was shining brightly, and I went for a walk along the lake.
- before or after a dependent clause in a sentence.
  Although my door was shut, I could still hear the radio.
- before and after clauses that could be in parentheses.
  When my dog barked, which he doesn't usually do, I checked the door.
- between two or more adjectives that are modifying a noun.
  the hot, bright sun   *the old, green, wool mittens*
- between items in a list or series.
  I need to buy shampoo, toothpaste, and tissue.
- to separate spoken words from the rest of the sentence.
  Janice asked, "When are you coming over?"
  "I'll be there early," he replied.

> **TIP**
>
> When you revise your writing, read your work out loud. Listen for the natural pauses and then put in commas where you pause.

WRITING SENSE

- after the greeting in a friendly letter and after the closing.
  Dear Elena,   Sincerely,
- following a person's name before his or her title.
  Pierre Trudeau, the former prime minister, will speak.
- in dates.
  July 1, 1967   Tuesday, May 22nd
- after exclamations that do not express a strong emotion.
  Well, here we are.   Oh dear, where did I put my book?
- before and after words such as *however*, *indeed*, and *obviously*.
  I think, however, that we should go home.

Dashes

A **dash** (—) separates one part of a sentence from the rest of the sentence. Dashes let the reader know there is going to be a break in the flow of the sentence.

- Dashes show a sudden break in a sentence, as if a thought has been interrupted. Commas can be used this way as well, but dashes are stronger.
  Jason—he's my older brother—refused to go camping with me.
- Dashes show a sudden break in speech.
  "Where are—" Deanna began and then stopped suddenly.
- Dashes are used to introduce an explanation or list. The dash takes the place of phrases such as *namely*, *that is*, and *in other words*.
  Stefan has three favourite pastimes—watching television shows, playing video games, and surfing the Net.

> **TIP**
> Dashes are powerful punctuation marks, so use them carefully. You may want to use commas or rewrite the sentence to avoid using dashes, especially in formal writing.

Ellipses

An **ellipsis** or ellipses points (…) are a series of three dots that show that something has been left out.

- One or more words have been left out of a quotation.
  The story The Hockey Sweater *by Roch Carrier starts "The winters of my childhood were long, long seasons. We lived in three places—the school, the church, and the skating rink—but our real life was on the skating rink."*
  This could be shortened to
  "The winters of my childhood were long, long seasons. We lived in three places…but our real life was on the skating rink."
- A sentence or thought has been left unfinished.
  I stopped to think…but no thoughts would come.

Exclamation Marks

An **exclamation mark** (!) is used at the end of a sentence to show surprise, enthusiasm, disbelief, urgency, or another strong emotion. Exclamation marks are also called exclamation points. Exclamation marks

- punctuate a sentence, a phrase, or a word that expresses surprise or a strong emotion
  We've finally finished!   Well done!   Stop!
- replace a question mark when the tone of the question is very strong
  What are you doing now!

Parentheses and Brackets

- **Parentheses** ( ) are used to add information that is not essential to the meaning of the sentence without changing the structure of the sentence.
  After the game (our last of the season), we are going to Keeghan's house.
- **Square brackets** [ ] are used to add information that was not included by the author.
  She grew up in Paris [Ontario], but moved to Montreal.
- Parentheses and brackets are not introduced by any punctuation.

TIP

If ellipses points are used at the end of a sentence, include the period so that there will be four dots.

One of Shakespeare's most famous lines is "To be or not to be…."

TIP

Don't overuse exclamation marks or they won't mean anything special to your reader.

TIPS

Parentheses and dashes are used the same way. Choose the one you prefer. Some people think the dash is more noticeable, so they use it to make the information inside stand out.

WRITING SENSE

Periods

A **period** (.) shows that something is finished.

- Periods end sentences. *I left my lunch here and now it's gone.*
- Some abbreviations end with a period. If the abbreviation uses the first letter of each word, the period goes after each letter. *Can.   Dr.   B.A.   B.C.* However, many abbreviations are now being spelled without any periods. Often you can find both spellings. *U.N.* or *UN*
- Periods go after the initials in someone's name. Usually no space is left between the initials. *P.E. Trudeau   W.C. Fields*

> **TIP**
> Periods go inside quotation marks: *She said, "That's my house."*

> **TIP**
> A request (an indirect question) ends with a period: *Would you go to the gym, please.*

Question Marks

A **question mark** (?) lets readers know that the sentence they have just read is a question.

- A question mark ends a sentence that asks a direct question.
  What time is it?   Where is my hat?
- Question marks are placed inside quotation marks, parentheses, and dashes.
  After a few minutes, he asked "What's your name?"

Quotation Marks

Quotation marks (" ") are punctuation marks that show that someone is speaking, or that the information inside is a title.

- Quotation marks show direct speech.
  "What's that?" he said.
  "I think," Shauna replied, "it's only a dog."
- All quotations end in punctuation (a comma, period, question mark, and so on) and are introduced by a comma when they come after phrases such as *he said* and *she replied*.
- For a direct quotation inside a direct quotation, use single quotation marks.
  "And then he told me, 'I've flown a plane,'" Asad said.
- The titles of songs, poems, short stories, magazine and newspaper articles, and essays are surrounded by quotation marks.
  "In the Next War" by Robert Priest is my favourite poem.
- Quotation marks always come in pairs. In the Canadian style of writing, the periods and commas are put inside the quotation marks.

> **TIP**
> Quotation marks are not used for indirect quotations—quotations that do not reproduce exactly what was said. Indirect quotations are often introduced by the word *that*: *Hari said that he was coming tonight.*

Semicolons

A **semicolon** (;) is similar to a period and a comma. They all separate different parts of a sentence. Some people think of semicolons as weak periods or strong commas. A semicolon can't end a sentence like a period, but it can identify major sections of a sentence.

- Semicolons go between main clauses that don't have a conjunction (a connecting word such as *and, or,* or *but*).
  The giant panda is endangered; its habitats are disappearing.
- Semicolons separate items in a list, if the items are long phrases or clauses. Generally the last item will follow a conjunction such as *and, or,* or *but*.
  On my vacation I went to a baseball game in Montreal; camping with my uncle in Temagami; whitewater rafting on the Ottawa River; and rock climbing along the Niagara Escarpment.
- Semicolons are put before words and phrases that introduce examples or lists, such as *for example, namely, for instance, i.e., e.g., as,* and *that is*; and before clauses that start with words such as *moreover, however, also, therefore,* and *consequently*.
- Often it is clearer to use a semicolon rather than a comma to separate a long dependent clause from the rest of the sentence.
  We worked hard designing, building, and painting the model; although we didn't know who would use it.

Slashes

- The **slash** (/) shows that there is choice.
  We can choose a book and/or a magazine to read.
- The slash also separates items that are usually on separate lines, such as lines of poetry. When these lines have been run together in writing, each original line is separated by a slash.
  Tiger, Tiger, burning bright/In the forests of the night,/What immortal hand or eye,/Could frame thy fearful symmetry?
- A slash is also used in abbreviations and ratios.
  km/h (kilometres per hour)   c/o (in care of)
  We have a 50/50 chance of winning.   3/4

Spelling

Abbreviations

Abbreviations are the shortened forms of words or phrases. Abbreviations are formed by dropping letters from a word. Some abbreviations have periods at the end; others do not. (Through common practice, the period is slowly disappearing from abbreviations.)

- Sentences should not begin with an abbreviation. Either reword the sentence or write the word out in full.
- The first time you write an abbreviation in a piece of writing, use the long form with the abbreviation following in parentheses—*United Nations (UN)*. Then you can use the abbreviation throughout the rest of the piece.
- Try not to use too many abbreviations at once. It makes the sentence harder to read.

Here are some common abbreviations.

Countries

CAN/Can.	Canada
US/U.S.A.	United States

Days

Fri.	Friday
Mon.	Monday
Sat.	Saturday
Sun.	Sunday
Thurs.	Thursday
Tues.	Tuesday
Wed.	Wednesday

General

A.D.	(Latin, *anno Domini*) in the year of our Lord
a.m.	(Latin, *ante meridiem*) before noon
apt.	apartment
ASAP	as soon as possible
B.C.	before Christ
c. or ca	(Latin, *circa*) around, about
CD	compact disk
c/o	in care of
C.O.D./c.o.d.	cash on delivery
dept.	department
Dr.	Doctor
e.g.	(Latin, *exempli gratia*) for example
et al.	(Latin, *et alii*) and others
etc.	(Latin, *et cetera*) and so forth
f/x or fx	special effects
FYI	for your information
govt.	government
i.e.	(Latin, *id est*) that is
incl.	including

TOOL KIT

Jr.	Junior
Ltd.	limited
max.	maximum
min.	minimum
misc.	miscellaneous
MLA	Member of the Legislative Assembly
MP	Member of Parliament
MPP	Member of Provincial Parliament
Mt.	Mount
N/A	not available or not applicable
no.	number
p./pg.	page
PC	personal computer
PIN	personal identification number
p.m.	(Latin, *post meridiem*) after noon
P.M.	Prime Minister
pop.	population
P.S.	postscript
RCMP	Royal Canadian Mounted Police
ref.	reference
RN	registered nurse
RSVP	(French, *répondez s'il vous plait*) please answer
SASE	self-addressed stamped envelope
Sr.	Senior
TBA/t.b.a.	to be announced
temp.	temperature or temporary
TV/t.v.	television
UFO	unidentified flying object
UN	United Nations
UNESCO	United Nations Educational, Scientific, and Cultural Organization
UNICEF	United Nations Children's Fund
vet.	veterinarian or veteran
VIP	very important person
vol.	volume
V.P.	vice-president
WWW	World Wide Web

Months

Apr.	April
Aug.	August
Dec.	December
Feb.	February
Jan.	January
Mar.	March
Nov.	November
Oct.	October
Sept.	September

Provinces

AB/Alta.	Alberta
BC/B.C.	British Columbia
MB/Man.	Manitoba
NB/N.B.	New Brunswick
NF/Nfld.	Newfoundland
NS/N.S.	Nova Scotia
NT/N.W.T.	Northwest Territories
ON/Ont.	Ontario
PE/P.E.I.	Prince Edward Island
PQ/Que.	Quebec
SK/Sask.	Saskatchewan
YT/Y.T.	Yukon Territory

Street Names

AVE/Ave.	Avenue
BLVD/Blvd.	Boulevard
CRES/Cres.	Crescent
CT/Crt.	Court
DR/Dr.	Drive
RD/Rd.	Road
RR/R.R.	Rural Route
ST/St.	Street

Alternate Spellings

When reading books, magazines, and newspapers from the United States, you might notice that some words have different spellings than we commonly use in Canada.

- Words such as *honour, colour,* and *neighbour* end in **or** rather than **our** (U.S.: *color*).
- Words such as *centre, metre,* and *fibre* end in **er** rather than **re** (U.S.: *center*).
- In words such as *traveller, labelling, signalled, jewellery,* and *woollen,* **one l** rather than a **double l** has been added before the suffix (U.S.: *traveler*).
- Some words have a **z** rather than an **s** in words such as *analyse, paralyse,* and *cosy* (U.S.: *analyze*).
- Other Canadian spellings are *storey* (U.S.: *story*), as in a *two-storey building*; *grey* (U.S.: *gray*); *catalogue* (U.S.: *catalog*); and *cheque* (U.S.: *check*).
- Words such as *licence* (noun) and *license* (verb) have only one spelling (U.S.: *license* for noun and verb); and *practice* (noun) and *practise* (verb) (U.S.: *practice* for noun and verb).

Commonly Misspelled Words

Some words are just hard to spell. The word may have a silent letter (*sign, island*), double letters (*embarrass*), or a combination of letters that make an unexpected sound (*weight*). Keep an eye out for these words in your writing.

a**n**swer	co**mm**i**tt**ee	impo**ss**ible	unti**l**
a**pp**ear**ance**	c**ough**	o**cc**ur	vacu**um**
argu**m**ent	embar**rass**	rhy**thm**	w**ei**ght
a**th**lete	en**ough**	sand**w**ich	W**edne**sday
autu**mn**	exer**cise**	sci**e**nce	
begi**nn**ing	famili**ar**	sep**a**rate	
bel**ie**ve	February	simil**ar**	
bought	fri**e**nd	sincer**e**ly	
bu**si**ness	government	su**rr**ounded	
bu**sy**	h**eight**	tomo**rr**ow	

Contractions

Contractions are two words combined into one word. An apostrophe takes the place of part of one word; for example, the contraction of *do not* is *don't* and the contraction of *they had* is *they'd*. When you write contractions, think about which two words make up the word you want. The following are common contractions listed under the word that has been shortened.

Not	Will	Have	Would/Had	Is/Has	Are
aren't	I'll	I've	I'd	he's	you're
can't	we'll	you've	you'd	she's	we're
couldn't	you'll	they've	he'd	it's	they're
didn't	he'll	could've	she'd	that's	who're
don't	she'll	should've	we'd	there's	
hadn't	it'll	might've	they'd	who's	**Am**
hasn't	one'll	who've	it'd	here's	I'm
haven't	they'll	there've	there'd	one's	
isn't	these'll	would've	what'd	what's	**Us**
mustn't	those'll	what've	who'd		let's
shouldn't	that'll		that'd		
wasn't	this'll	**Other Contractions**			
weren't	what'll	o'clock			
won't	who'll	jack-o'-lantern			
wouldn't	won't	'twas (it was)			

Homophones and Homographs

People are sometimes confused about the difference between homophones and homographs.

- **Homophones** are words that sound the same, but have different spellings and meanings. (Hint: *Phone* comes from a word meaning *sound*.)
  dear a term of affection   **deer** an animal with antlers
- **Homographs** are words that are spelled the same, but have different meanings and sometimes different pronunciations. (Hint: *Graph* comes from a word meaning *writing*.)
  bow a **bow** and arrow   **bow** the **bow** of a ship

> **TIP**
>
> When you are revising and editing your writing, check for homophones. Have you used the appropriate one?

Here are some common homophones to watch for.

ate/eight	pain/pane	side/sighed
bear/bare	pair/pear/pare	sight/site/cite
beat/beet	pale/pail	size/sighs
blue/blew	plane/plain	some/sum
cent/sent/scent	pour/pore	son/sun
cheap/cheep	principal/principle	Sunday/sundae
dear/deer	rain/reign/rein	they're/their/there
fair/fare	raise/rays	tied/tide
for/four/fore	read/reed	to/too/two
grown/groan	ring/wring	warn/worn
hair/hare	road/rode/rowed	way/weigh
here/hear	roll/role	weak/week
its/it's	sale/sail	we'd/weed
main/mane	seam/seem	whose/who's
night/knight	seas/sees/seize	write/right
no/know	see/sea	you're/your
one/won	sell/cell	

Numbers

Writers are sometimes confused about whether to use numerals or to spell out **numbers** in their writing.

- Numbers from one to nine are usually written as words while numbers 10 and over are usually written as numerals.
  two   25   25000
  Exception: Numbers being compared should be written in the same way.
  The grades in this school range from 7 to 12.
- Use a combination of numbers and words for very large numbers.
  20 million   2 billion
- Use words, not numbers, to begin a sentence.
  Thirty-thousand fans attended the opening game.

Spelling Strategies

Once you've written your piece and revised and edited it, you should make sure there are no spelling mistakes. Correct spelling ensures that your reader will understand what you've written. Think about these suggestions and strategies for becoming a better speller.

1 Create a personal speller. Make a list of words you know you have trouble spelling. Use your list when you proofread.

2 Try using memory tricks. It could be a phrase, a statement, or a rhyme:
   – Use **i** before **e** except after **c** and in words that rhyme with **ay** (*believe, receive, eight*). **Exceptions:** *weird, height, species, seize, foreign*.
   – An **e**, **i**, or **y** after a **c** or **g** usually makes a soft **c** or **g** sound (*pace/pact, ginger/gate*). **Exceptions:** *get, tiger, gift, giggle*.

3 Study words that you find hard to spell.
   - Look at the word as you say it out loud. Spell it out loud.
   - Write the word, saying each letter as you write it.
   - Read the word out loud again.
   - Check to make sure you've spelled the word correctly.
   - Cover the word and write it again saying each letter as you write it. Check your spelling.

4 Think about related words. Many words belong to word families, for example, *knowledge* and *acknowledge*. Related words can give you hints about how to spell the words you don't know.

5 Use a dictionary.

Proofreading Tips

- Start with the last line of your writing and read from the bottom to the top. This will help you to concentrate on each word. Remember that you are not reading for meaning, only for spelling.
- Put a line through each misspelling and write the correct word above it.
- If you aren't sure about a word, circle it. Once you've checked the whole piece, you can go back and check these words in a dictionary.
- Ask a classmate to read your piece for spelling.

Word Power

Much of the beauty of writing comes from the words we use. To be an effective writer you need to choose the right words to convey your meaning.

Antonyms

Antonyms are two words that are opposite in meaning (*up/down, big/small, tall/short, sunny/cloudy*).

- Many writers use antonyms to emphasize a point or add power to their writing. The contrast between antonyms, such as *fast* and *slow*, can add humour, intrigue, or contrast. *The **fast** car slowed down.*
- You can also use antonyms in your writing to say the same thing in a different way. Instead of saying: *Sam was too short to reach the shelf*, you could write: *The shelf was too high for Sam to reach.*

Appropriate Language

Be conscious of the type of language that you use in your writing. Watch for stereotypes, unnecessary violence, and sexist language.

1. Avoid making your characters stereotypes. A stereotype is an oversimplified and usually overdone character type, such as the bully, the villain, or the damsel in distress. In essays or reports, avoid any language that might portray an individual in a stereotyped or prejudiced way.
2. Violence is overused by inexperienced writers. Avoid violence unless it is vital to the story, and instead concentrate on revealing the events and characters.
3. Avoid sexist language. Sexist language implies that one sex is better or more important in some way than the other and is unfair to both sexes.
   - In the past, the pronouns *he, him,* or *his* were used to refer to both males and females as a group, or used instead of the female pronouns, even when the gender of the person in the sentence wasn't clear. To correct this, rewrite the sentence to avoid the use of a pronoun, or put the pronoun into the plural—*they, them,* or *their*—making sure the verb corresponds properly.

Words to Avoid	Replace With
businessman	executive, business person
chairman	chairperson
fireman	firefighter
housewife	homemaker
mailman	mail carrier
man, mankind	human beings, people
salesman	sales person
stewardess	flight attendant
waitress	server, worker
workman	employee

Commonly Misused Words

Sometimes we aren't sure we have used the right word with the right meaning in our writing. Some words are used in similar ways or they sound alike so it's hard to decide if we've used the proper word. Check these words or phrases when you use them in your writing.

Words	Usage	Examples
accept except	*Accept* is a verb meaning receive. *Except* is a preposition meaning to exclude someone or something.	I **accepted** her invitation to lunch. Everyone **except** Tony went to the game.
affect effect	*Affect* is a verb meaning to cause a change. *Effect* is a noun meaning result.	A headache **affected** my performance on the test. The car crash left lasting **effects.**
among between	Use *among* when talking about three or more things. Use *between* when talking about two things.	Jane, Wendy, and I had a discussion **among** ourselves. I can't decide **between** new shoes or a new coat.
amount number	Use *amount* with general quantities. Use *number* when referring to specific quantities and things that can be measured or counted.	I ate a large **amount** of chips for lunch. The **number** of parks in my neighbourhood is quite small.
bring take	*Bring* means moving toward the speaker. *Take* means to carry away.	Please **bring** me the book. **Take** the garbage outside.
can may	*Can* means having the ability to do something. *May* means asking for permission to do something.	I **can** hold my breath underwater for one minute. **May** I close this door? It's drafty in here.
compare to compare with	When you use *compare to*, focus on similarities. When you use *compare with*, focus on similarities and differences.	My mother likes to **compare** me **to** my sister. Jane wants to **compare** her newspaper article **with** mine.
conscious conscience	*Conscious* means alert. *Conscience* means having a sense of right and wrong.	I wasn't **conscious** of the time passing. My **conscience** bothered me after I broke my brother's favourite computer game.
desert dessert	A *desert* is a dry, barren region. *Dessert* is a food such as fruit or cake that is served at the end of a meal.	There aren't many trees in the **desert.** My favourite **dessert** is chocolate cake.
different from different than	*Different than* is incorrect. Use *different from*.	My idea of a great movie is **different from** my best friend's.
don't doesn't	*Don't* is the contraction of do not. *Doesn't* is the contraction of does not.	**Don't** forget your lunch. He **doesn't** have the car keys.

Words	Usage	Examples
farther further	*Farther* refers to geographical distance. *Further* refers to quantity or degree.	Hamilton is **farther** from Toronto than Oakville is. **Further** tests are necessary.
fewer less	*Fewer* describes something that can be measured or counted. *Less* describes something that you can't count.	I had **fewer** mistakes on this test than I had on the last one. I get **less** and **less** time to get my work done.
good well	*Good* is an adjective. *Well* is an adverb.	I had a **good** time at the festival. I am not feeling **well**.
lie lay	*Lie* means to rest or to recline. *Lay* means to put or to place.	I am going to **lie** down for an hour. **Lay** my coat on the chair by the door, please.
loan lend	*Loan* is a noun, not a verb. Use *lend* as the verb.	I need a **loan** to buy a new car. Will you **lend** me $10 until tomorrow?
maybe may be	*Maybe* is an adverb meaning possibly. *May be* is a verb phrase.	**Maybe** I'll go to the movies on Saturday. I **may be** visiting my relatives next month.
quote quotation	*Quote* is a verb. *Quotation* is a noun.	Don't **quote** me on that. Which **quotation** did you use?
real really	*Real* is an adjective. Don't use *real* as an adverb. *Really* is an adverb.	Is that ring **real** gold? I worked **really** hard last summer.
stationary stationery	*Stationary* means a fixed position. *Stationery* refers to writing paper, envelopes, pens, and pencils.	I have a **stationary** bike. I just bought new **stationery**.
who whom	*Who* is a relative pronoun used as a subject. *Whom* is a relative pronoun used as an object.	**Who** is at the door? From **whom** did you get that book?

Synonyms

A **synonym** is a word that has the same or almost the same meaning as another word. *Courage* and *bravery*, and *terrible* and *horrible* are synonyms.

- As you revise your writing, look for words that you are overusing. It may be possible to replace some of these words with their synonyms. But be careful. Sometimes using a synonym will change the meaning slightly, since very few synonyms have exactly the same meaning.
- Dictionaries will often include synonyms at the end of an entry.
- A thesaurus is the best place to find synonyms. Remember to check the meaning of the new word you have used in the dictionary to make sure it is really the word you want to use.

Using Dictionaries

The words in a dictionary are called entries and they appear in alphabetical order. Each page of the dictionary has two guide words at the top of the page that you can use to help you find the entry you're looking for.

Entries usually include information showing
- the spelling of the word
- how it's divided into syllables
- how it's pronounced
- its definition(s)
- its part of speech (for example, noun, verb, adjective, and so on)
- other forms of the word, such as the plural
- examples of how the word is used in a sentence
- synonyms
- the origin of the word (called etymology)

Some dictionaries offer more than spelling and meaning.

- Word origin dictionaries provide detailed information about the origin and history of the words they list.
- Rhyming dictionaries list words according to rhyming patterns.
- Picture dictionaries provide pictures of the words.

bread (bred) n., v.—n. **1** a food made of flour or meal mixed with milk or water and, usually, yeast, that is kneaded, shaped into loaves and baked. **2** food; livelihood. **3** Slang. money.

Using Thesauruses

A thesaurus is a reference book with a list of words that have similar meanings to the word you looked up. Check a thesaurus when you want to avoid using the same word over and over. Choose the word that is closest to what you mean. Here's how to find the word you're looking for in a thesaurus.

1. Look in the index for your word. The index listing for the word *welcome* might look like this:
   welcome *reception* 299 n., *greet* 884 v., *applaud* 923 v.
   The words listed in italics have similar meanings to *welcome*. The page number is given along with the word's part of speech.

2. Go to that page in the main part of the thesaurus and read through the entry for word suggestions.

3. Double-check the word in the dictionary to make sure it really means what you think it does.

WRITING SENSE

Index

abbreviations, 74, 181
abstract nouns, 160
action, 134
action verbs, 161
active voice, 162
adjectives, 162–163
adverbs, 163
advertisements, print, 83–88
advertising, 82, 150
alibis, 31
alliteration, 92, 93, 134, 140
anecdotes, 130, 134
antagonists, 134
antonyms, 187
apostrophes, 175
appendix, 156
appropriate language, 187
atmosphere, 135
audience, 12
audio-visual sources, 158

bibliographies, 155, 156
biographical dictionaries, 157
brackets, 178
brainstorming, 9

capitalization, 102, 104, 175
captions, 135
CD-ROMs, 53, 157
characterization, 136
characters, 42, 116, 135
charts, 11
clauses, 167
cliff-hangers, 136
climax, 145
close-ended questions, 59
colons, 118, 176
command sentences, 110
commas, 176
common nouns, 160
comparatives, 164
comparisons, 139
complex sentences, 168
compound nouns, 160
compound sentences, 168
compound subjects, 170
conclusions, 137
concrete nouns, 160
conflict, 137
conjunctions, 164
contents page, 156
contractions, 74, 184
couplets, 87, 92, 95–97

dashes, 177
demographics, 61
dependent clauses, 167
descriptive adjectives, 162
descriptive paragraphs, 67, 172
dialogue, 43, 138
diaries, 21
dictionaries, 190
directories, 157
direct quotations, 68
drafts, 14, 17, 19
drama, 113
dramatic irony, 141

e-mail, 89, 125, 158
editing, 16, 19
editing symbols, 16
ellipses, 178
encyclopedias, 157
endings of articles, 137
exaggeration, 138
exclamation marks, 178
explanatory paragraphs, 54, 174
exposition, 145
expository paragraphs, 174
expressions, transitional, 62, 168

falling action, 145
fantasy stories, 33–38
final draft, 19
first-person point of view, 123, 124, 146
flashback, 139
foreshadowing, 31, 139
foreword, 156
formal language, 139
format, 12
formatting, 38
found poetry, 101–104
free verse, 94, 149
free writing, 10
friendly letters, 76–81
future tense, 162

glossary, 156
grammar, 160
graphic organizers, 10
graphs, 61

helping verbs, 161
homographs, 47, 49, 184
homophones, 47, 49, 184–185
humour, 44-49
hyperbole, 139

ideas for writing, 9
idioms, 46, 48, 140
imagery, 67, 140
independent clauses, 167
index, 156
indirect quotations, 68
informal language, 129, 141
instructional paragraphs, 174
instructions, 107
interjections, 165
interviews, 158
introduction of a book, 156
irony, 141

jargon, 55, 142
jingles, 89–91
jokes, 45–47
journals, 22–25
juxtaposition, 85, 142

layout, 69, 87, 105
leads, 67, 142
letters, 76, 123-125
letters to the editor, 121–125
libraries, 156
limited point of view, 146
limiting adjectives, 163
linking verbs, 161

mail, electronic, 89, 125, 158
main clauses, 167
metaphors, 130, 140, 143
meter, poetic, 148–149
misspelled words, 183
mood, 135
multiple-choice questions, 59
mysteries, 28–32

narration, 143
narrative paragraphs, 79, 173
narrative writing, 27
narrators, 117, 143
non-fiction books, 156
non-racist language, 187
non-sexist language, 187
nouns, 99, 160
noun/verb agreement, 160
numbers, 185

object, 166
onomatopoeia, 92, 140, 144
open-ended questions, 59
outlines, 13

paragraphs, 37, 171
    descriptive, 67, 172
    explanatory, 54, 174
    instructional, 174
    narrative, 79, 173
    persuasive, 173
parentheses, 178
parts of a sentence, 166–168
parts of speech, 160–165
passive voice, 162
past tense, 162
pen pals, 78
periods, 179
personal journals, 22
personal writing, 22–26
personification, 36, 140, 144
persuasive writing, 120, 173
phrases, 166
plot, 145
plural verbs, 162
poetry, 94–105
    couplets and quatrains, 95–97
    found, 101–104
    free verse, 94, 149
point form, 147
point of view, 124, 146
possessive nouns, 160
postscript, 78
pourquoi tales, 39–43
predicate, 166
preface, 156
prepositions, 165
present tense, 162
print advertisements, 83–88
profiles, 63–69
pronouns, 161
proofreading, 16, 186
proper nouns, 160
protagonists, 42, 147
publishing, 16
punctuation, 104, 131
    apostrophes, 175
    brackets, 178
    colons, 176
    commas, 176
    dashes, 177
    ellipses, 178
    exclamation marks, 178
    parentheses, 178
    periods, 179
    question marks, 179
    quotation marks, 179
    semicolons, 180
    slashes, 180
puns, 45, 46, 147
purpose, 12

quatrains, 95, 97
question marks, 179
questionnaires, 59–60
questions, 59
quotation marks, 179
quotations, 68

racist language, 187
reader's theatre scripts, 114–119
reference sources, 15, 156
repetition, 148
reports, 53
research, 50, 154
research reports, 51–56
resolution, 145
revising, 15, 18
rhyme, 92, 97, 148
rhyming couplets, 92
rhyming patterns, 97
rhythm, 92, 97, 99, 149
riddles, 45
rising action, 145
rules, 106–112
run-on sentences, 32, 169

salutations, 76
scripts, 113, 138
second-person point of view, 146
semicolons, 180
sentences,
    command, 110
    complex, 168
    compound, 168
    fragments, 169
    run-on, 32, 169
    simple, 168
    styles, 86, 131, 170
setting, 149
sexist language, 187
signatures, 76
similes, 139, 140, 150
simple sentences, 168
singular verbs, 162
slashes, 180
slogans, 86, 92, 150
speeches, 126–132
spelling, 181, 183
    abbreviations, 181–182
    alternate, 183
    contractions, 184
    homographs, 184
    homophones, 184–185
    numbers, 185
    proofreading, 186
    strategies, 186
square brackets, 178
stanzas, 98, 104, 149

statements, 109
statistics, 61
stereotypes, 187
subject, 166, 170
subordinate clauses, 167
summary, 137
superlatives, 164
surveys, 57–62, 158
suspense, 31, 151
symbols, 151
synonyms, 189

table of contents, 156
tense, 162
thank-you notes, 71–75
theme, 151
thesaurus, 190
third-person point of view, 124, 146
tone, 25, 86, 152
topics, 12
transitional expressions, 62, 168
tree diagrams, 10

usage, 160

verb tense, 162
verbal irony, 141
verbs, 161–162
voice, 12, 152, 162

webs, 10
words, 187
    commonly misused, 188–189
    jargon, 55
    sound-alike, 47
    sounds, 144
words that confuse, 183, 188
World Wide Web, 53, 158
writing,
    advertisements, 82
    drama, 113
    humour, 44
    instructions, 106
    messages, 70
    narrative, 27
    personal, 21
    persuasive, 120, 173
    poetry, 94
    research, 50
writing folders, 9
writing formats, 20
Writing Process, 8